D0700316

Stories on the Wind

Copyright ©2018 Gardner McKay

Cover design by
David Madigan Artist's website: www.davemadigan.ie

Stories on the Wind
Volume II
A collection of short stories
Is published by
Shiptree Publications - Honolulu, Hawaii 96822 USA

All Rights Reserved.

No part of this book may be reproduced or transmitted in any form or by any means,
electronic, or mechanical - including on-line, digital, photocopy, recording, or any information
storage and retrieval system now known or to be invented - except for the inclusion in a
review, without permission in writing from the publisher.

Additional copies of this book may be ordered directly at
www.CreateSpace.com

McKay; Gardner
Stories on the Wind
Shiptree Publications, Honolulu, Hawaii ©2018
ISBN:978-0-9966682-4-8

First Edition published June 2018
Printed in the United States of America

Stories on the Wind

Volume II

An anthology of short stories by

Gardner McKay

Shiptree Publications / Hawaii 2018

Other works by Gardner McKay

Short Stories
Stories on the Wind
Volume 1

Memoir
Journey Without a Map

Novels
Trompe L'Oeil
Toyer: A Novel of Suspense
The Kinsman

Novella
Ten, Bloomsbury Square

Stage Plays
Toyer
Sea Marks
Masters of the Sea
Untold Damage
In Order of Appearance

Teleplays
Untold Damage
Sea Marks

Table of Contents

INTRODUCTION

෨

In 1986, with our house in Beverly Hills leased for the long term, Gardner and I and our young daughter, Liza, took a house in London. While she attended school there, we settled in to enjoy another culture, distant and quite different from the one we were used to in California. We spent several months there before retreating to the Canary Islands to escape the gloomy weather and experience a completely different environment. But we soon realized that Gardner's need to write and Liza's educational future would best be served by living in the US, so we decided to move to back to Hawaii, where Gardner and I first met. We found a rental on O'ahu across from the beach in Kailua and Gardner found a small office nearby where he could work without interruption.

A few years later we purchased a property in Koko Head, an ancient tuff cone on the side of the dormant volcano known as Koko Crater. Soon after moving in, Gardner built a small office on the property and named it *Hale ka'ao,* which means "story house."

"It isolates me in an isolated place," he explained. "An island on an island."

Over the next decade he wrote tens of thousands of words that eventually comprised four novels, dozens of short stories, poems, song lyrics, plays and screenplays. But as time passed the small space became cramped and he found it increasingly difficult to organize his work there.

For many years various friends and acquaintances had suggested he write an autobiography of his richly adventurous journey through life, but he felt he had more important work to do.

Then, in early January 2000, Gardner was diagnosed with terminal cancer. After returning from intensive treatments at UCLA Medical Center, he decided it was a good time to write that memoir. Now he had a true deadline. Knowing he could not take on such a task without adequate space to lay out all his journals and copious notes, as well as the memorabelia he'd accumulated over seven decades, he realized he needed a larger, more suitable space than the *Hale ka'ao* offered. And so he designed an expansion and hired a well-reputed builder to bring it to life.

I have included *My Dream House* in this collection as the prologue because I feel it is relevant. It is the story of a dying writer who needs an appropriate space to create his last book, a story of greed and deception and a scam that brings him nothing but misery at a time of most extreme difficulty. It is also relevant because all the stories that follow were written by Gardner in this place…

Madeleine McKay

PROLOGUE:
MY DREAM HOUSE

❧

A true story.

There she stands. My dream house. My little San Simeon. I've waited a lifetime. But like San Simeon, it stands unfinished on its slab where it has stood for months.

My dream house was never meant to look like other dream houses. Small by any standards, it was meant to be little more than a shell. One-story, one room thirty feet long, twelve feet wide, set in a depression on the property. Two french doors east and west, two vents. Four casement windows set to capture the trades along the north side. A thirty foot blank wall. No view, no telephone, no plumbing, cement floor, two ceiling fans, the luxury was to be air an conditioner to keep pages from sticking to my forearms. Inside it would be cool and gloomy. Perfect. A copper roof. A belfry set in its center for light and air, it would probably resemble a country schoolhouse. And that's it. Not a fabulous house. My house *Hale ka'ao,* my new writing house. My extension of Virginia Woolf's "Room of One's Own," her Edwardian plea proclaiming the need to create your own space. It was all I wanted. My dreams are attainable. Or are they?

From my old *Hale ka'ao,* where I sit now, have come hundreds of stories and chapters of novels that I read aloud each Sunday and Monday nights on "Stories On The Wind," my KHPR Public Radio program. The old *hale* now resembles a cave of loose paper. Every word is in sight. Every manuscript. All in various drafts, accompanied by multitudinous stacks of pages labeled ideas handwritten notes on scraps one inch across to pages eight by eleven inches. I built this hale with a friend in a gully on the property. It has floor space of maybe 60 square feet and as I wrote in it over the years it grew smaller and smaller, slowly filling up with a detritus of words, each one a small debt owed to its completion, each continually trying to snare my attention. It is where the vast majesty of the bug kingdom convenes each evening. Early this year I decided I needed a change. A new hale. It would not be a conceit. Not some spoiled brat indulgence. A work house. A stockroom where these manuscripts of plays stories novels, articles novellas scripts might be sorted out read and refined. I was blessed to be able to borrow the money from a friend who believed it was a good idea.

All houses are built from love. If not from love, from hope, from excitement, from anticipation, or, if not from one of the above, by developers. Purchasing a house may be an exciting experience, but the excitement is diminished by vivacious Realtors and clusters of sycophants who force us to run gauntlets of outstretched palms (so <u>that's</u> what those blank-looking offices are for.)

But building your own house. Ah, there's the difference, it is only between your dream and your builder. Ever since *Homo Erectus* set a circle of stones in place one million nine hundred thousand years ago, we have been building habitats for ourselves with various levels of zest. I imagine there may once have been cave trading by Pleistocene Realtors, who knows, but creating one's own shelter represents arrival at a destination of well-being. Building contractors have always known this. Especially Don.

ENTER DON

A wise friend, call him Malcolm, recommended a contractor, call him Don. I liked Don. Forty something, Don had a gang haircut, fingertips missing on his left hand. Wide-eyed, swarthy, a demeanor that passes for ingenuous. His contractor's card called him a home medic. It failed to mention the word *criminal,* which is what Don is.

Malcolm had been completely taken in by Don, he knew nothing of his darker side. He had met him in a park, teaching martial arts to little boys, including his son. Malcolm properly pronounced it *kar-ra-tay* to me. He said that Don had been dealt some cruel cards, that the world had it in for him. People plotted against him, life had ganged up on him. His van had been vandalized. So had his son's. He had many small maladies. Malcolm listened to his story. He felt sorry for him and stored his van to get it off the street. It never occurred to Malcolm that contractors' vans are traditionally burglarized, not vandalized. To ignore the expensive tools and smash the windshields with a baseball bat and slash the four tires with a roofer's knife is a mark of displeasure. A displeasure that I was soon to share.

I realize now that Don was recommended not as a builder but as a personable victim who could use my help. A man who was good with children. I, too, was impressed by Don in a superficial way. A grubby charisma. He seemed adequately spiritual, earthy, willing. But those qualities have gone the way of firm handshakes, sincere eye contact, phrases like "trust me." Gone, too, with the gentleman's agreement.

I made a scale drawing, it included all my needs, and took it to an architect. Don made a bid of $28,500. Four to six weeks completion. Don asked only one thing in return for a job well done. What? When the house was built and I am happily at work in it, might I give Don a writing lesson? Gosh, yes. So little to ask for a job well done.

I accepted his terms and signed our contract and work began. That was July 5. The dream house still remains unfinished, standing in its underwear on its slab.

CONSTRUCTION BEGINS

7:00 am Saturday Don came to work with two men. Very impressive. The day before he had knocked on the neighbors' doors requesting their approval of an early start Saturday. Very considerate. He introduced me to the two men, 20'ish, one tall one short, but he never told me they were related to him. Odd. His sons. Call them Mutt and Jeff.

That day, Don saw me carrying my Nikon. He told me he always photographed his building projects and prepared a book of progress as a surprise for each homeowner. Just something he did for his own feeling of well-being. While he was speaking these words to me he knew that there would never be a book of photographs because there would never anything to photograph: he would never finish the job. He was enjoying his options as a con man. It was their last Saturday. I suppose con men require certain effects.

He did small favors for me to establish confidence. The boys willingly dug up three small fichus plants and planted them out of the way. He brought brochures and discussed shades for walls he would never paint. Even Abraham Lincoln, as a traveling law-yer, would borrow money when he came into a new town and quickly pay it back to establish credit.

The first payment on our contract, $6,500, "upon accept-ance," was due immediately. I realize now that I didn't know what that meant and never questioned it. Oops. Soon after, the next payment of $6,500 was for the pouring the foundation. Don inflated that payment to $9,500. The copper roof I'd got-ten from the mainland weighed ¼ what his contracted asphalt roof weighed. The house was light. Still, he said he needed two truckloads of concrete for the foundation. One came. The next $6,500 went for framing and roof sheathing and suddenly Don had $23,000.

$7,000 or so was left on the contract. What remained to be done was: sheathing and stuccoing the exterior walls, putting down the roof, bringing electrical power by trench from the main house, roughing in all the outlets and receptacles, hanging the drywall and taping it, painting the house, inside and out, three coats, buying and hanging french doors, buying and setting four vinyl windows, and four sets of jalousies for the belfry. And many other details that could not possibly be done for the remaining money. Time to go.

After ten days the job had slowed dramatically. Mutt or Jeff would show up and eat something. No nails left. We'd had 1500 bronze. Don had stolen them!

DON'S FALL

As the job came to a halt, one morning he arrived at 7:15 am and did not fall on the back steps. I was nearby. So was my wife who was just around the corner. Don removed a step from the back stairway, the second step from the bottom, then left.

Mysteriously, no one else had shown up that morning. It was as if they knew it was over. Half-an-hour later Don called from his car. My wife answered. "You should tighten those back steps," he said enigmatically. No mention of a fall. That afternoon he called again and told her that he'd fallen on his head. No one falls on his head. Especially *kar-ra-tay* people do not fall on their heads.

"Are you okay?" My wife asked him. He reported solemnly that the doctor at Kaiser had told him: "It's either a bruise or an aneurysm." Actually that's a laugh line.

I asked Malcolm to call Don and check into this non-injury. Don performed grammar-school-student tummy ache for him and Malcolm fell for it. He reported back to me that either Don was hurt or was a very great actor. I told him, a very great actor.

I called Don. Mutt answered.

"How's he doing?" Mutt told me Don was too drugged up to take my call.

"Any broken bones?" I asked.

"No."

The following day I called again. "Any broken bones?" I asked

"Maybe one or two," Mutt said. Another laugh line. The kids were learning.

The next day and for many days, Don would not take my calls. Through the wonders of electronics he could see I was calling. But somehow a week later I surprised him. I could hear the din of power tools in the background.

"Where are you?" I asked.

"I'm on my way to therapy at Kaiser."

Riding his circular saw.

But in a litigious world, it was enough to insure his freedom from our project and to pursue other projects full-time.

It took him a week or ten days for him to completely withdraw from the property. He had left the job site never to return, but to give the impression that it was only *See yaw* and not *Farewell*, he left behind a few tools he wasn't using. It is a touch like this that separates Don from the herd. Then one morning early, even though the gates were locked, someone managed to slip onto the property by walking down a neighbor's hillside and picked up whatever equipment he had left behind. But they didn't pick the piled concrete on the lawn, stacks of detritus, a vast assortment of fast food cups, plates, a mass of half-eaten food, decaying tacos, and, symbolically, a hammer.

THE SCAM FACTOR

In good faith, Don had taken nearly all the Dream House money. $6,500, $6,500, $6,500 from me, and the extra $2,620 for the phantom foundation expense. The out-of-proportion payments at the high end were for the simple labor, at the low end remained the expensive fine tuning work he wasn't planning to do anyway.

Fraud pure and simple. It is fraud to take money for a job

you never intend to complete. How can I be sure? Don had included the four vinyl windows in his bid. Vinyl windows must be ordered and paid for six-weeks in advance. The construction would take four to six weeks. The windows were never ordered. I asked him about them. He said he had called the window company and given them "attitude." No company, no call.

Don is a natural liar, a liar for all seasons. Chronic, congenital, compulsive. Under his tutelage Mutt and Jeff are coming along nicely. But they're no Don.

MY ILLNESS

I wasn't planning to tell Don about my illness. I never told anyone, only a couple of dozen people knew. But I wanted Don to understand. Last winter I had learned that I was pretty sick. Incurable, terminal, the full boat. I understand that all of us will be leaving some day, but news like this takes the vagueness out of our expiration date. And it is a banality among us in the know, our group, that we feel the need to "assemble our excrement." In my case it was not only emptying my wastebasket and neatening my papers, but more, it had to do with my work. A novel stacked in a corner of my *hale* housing geckos and spiders is a worthless stack of pages. To anyone but me. I am the warm solvent able to bring its essence to life. The only one who knows its meaning, goals, style, intentions. I have many, many such unfinished manuscripts.

I would never have mentioned my illness to Don but I wanted him on my side. I wanted him to know why the house was crucial to me and why I needed it as soon as possible. This was not some gazebo I had designed to toast sunset with a Martini, no, this was an essential part of my life, an extension of me, my heartbeat, my soul, my life. My work was in jeopardy and in desperate need of completion. Don listened gravely. He added a sentence to our contract: "Time is to be of the essence and every possible effort to be made to ensure a speedy project and," [In boldface italics:] *"**no additional projects to be constructed currently with Mr. McKay's workshop.**"* My man. Don was the real thing. He'd become part of my needs. Of course, in the time he was here, he kept taking on "additional projects."

The contract was quite wonderful but of course at the time I didn't recognize it as a primitive work of fiction. "No loud radios of foul language to be present upon job site. All efforts to leave clean and safe site upon the end of work each day to be of utmost concern. Framing to meet or exceed mainland framing standards." Yadda, yadda, yadda. None of it true.

But Don had broken my spirit. He had successfully derailed me.

THE C WORD

C stands for coward, an obsolete moral judgment. But Don is a coward. All thieves are cowards. Anyone is who takes money he has not earned. This goes for stock brokers, bankers, internet hustlers as well as burglars and armed robbers. No matter how respectable or dramatic the theft. There are other names for Don. He is borderline paranoiac, psychotic. He is angry.

In this era of lite morality it is up to the average citizen, us, to buckle up and become aware of how things work. The times have brought on a numbness where there used to be a chance to express trust. Buying a house once took a three page contract now it is closer to 300 pages because nobody trusts anyone. I paid $650 to Bishop Estate when I bought the land from Bishop Estate that my house sits on simply to insure that Bishop Estate really owned it! Stuff like that. To avoid any confusion, morality is gone with the wind.

THE SCUM FACTOR

But Don is a cut below scum. He may do you in, but he won't run, the law is kind to Don, he knows he can get away with it, he has found his niche.

Remarkably, a woman I'd never met telephoned me, the owner of her own wrecking company, and told me that she had simply requested her $2,500 deposit be returned for work that Don had not done. This at the time he was involved on my project. A week of silence was followed by Don's fax to her from a copy shop (he keeps unlisted addresses). It was a two-page bill "in the neighborhood of $7,400 in costs and lost earnings. Soft costs incurred for services rendered." Sound reasonable? She assured me there had been no services rendered. Among Don's charges was $2,250 for "specific costs" of Mutt and Jeff waiting around for three days. Then there was $2,800 to "Draw plans and specs" that did not exist. "The only reason," he wrote her, "that I haven't pressed you for before is as your friend, I see all the stress your under ..." That's pretty good of Don. He went on, "Please take sometime to review this and lets talk about how we could have gotten on so different of wavelengths. I will be on island until next week."

I'm sure Don has a judge-friendly account of his sudden departure from my property, too. I wonder how much he's not "pressing" me for. Don sure knows how to counter. And he'll justify what he does to you. I imagine he carries a photo of Johnny Cochran in his wallet.

R.I.C.O.

Belatedly, I called R.I.C.O. (pronounced *reeko)* an acronym for Regulated Industries Complaints Office. But R.I.C.O. only covers civil matters. Did I want to get my money back? Call a lawyer.

The operator was helpful and quick. Don is unlicensed. His license was revoked in 1992. He had done this before. He had half-a-dozen legal actions taken against him. He had been ordered to pay restitution four times. There were other complaints. The building complaints were "theft," "unfinished," "incompetent." It was clear that he was not qualified to have taken on this job.

INCOMPETENCE

Don probably couldn't have done it. Oddly enough, he's incompetent. His building skills can probably never catch up to his people skills.

He left behind him an unstable structure. A slab, studs, a partial roof. He did not connect the roof to the slab with hurricane straps. The framing plates were not bolted into the slab, they were nailed. The slab developed cracks. He did not leave space for the vents. He did not use galvanized joist hangers. He poked dozens of nails a full inch through the painted eaves. The 4 X 6s resting on the two front pillars were set four inches off center. Poor quality lumber was displayed. He left concrete slag on the lawn, killing the grass, piles of short ends, the garbage I mentioned.

THE POLICE

It was time to call the police. Two officers came by. They sat at the dining room table. Had they ever heard of Don? I mentioned his full name.

"I know him," the corporal said, "I've arrested him twelve times."

"For what?"

"You name it," the officer said. Drugs, burglary, et cetera.

"What about Mutt and Jeff?"

"They have rap sheets as long as my arm." And he held out a 34" sleeve.

In other words, the *kar-ra-tay* master's teachings had kicked in.

The officer said it would be difficult to get this out of a civil court action into criminal court. But Don already knew this.

Still, I wanted to be sure, so a week later I called the police again. A different officer came and sat at the table. He told me that the justice system in Hawaii was *f***ed.* That the criminal was better off than the good citizen. And Don's still out there doing people in and hasn't skipped a beat. Call him, he's in the Yellow Pages under Con.

THE LAW

I called a friend at the FBI who said that Don had committed fraud and should be put in jail. Don's intention from the beginning was to defraud me. This was not some dispute between homeowner and contractor. This was a criminal act.

I called the city prosecutor. In the most diplomatic way, he told me to give it up. I pressed him. He took all my project money, I said. Get yourself a lawyer.

This would be comedy except that it works for Don and the law is comfortable with him. Don's okay. In the eyes of the law Don's just a lovable scoundrel who's trying to get along. Litigation was made for Don. He uses the law the way a rapist uses an underground parking lot.

WHY IT HAPPENS

Our judicial system has gums, not teeth. They can bite but they only wet.

WHAT YOU CAN DO

1. If you intend to build, draw a measured sketch to scale of your proposed project. If it is more complex than a tool shed or a gazebo, bring in an architect.

2. Locate three builders, either through the architect, friends or the Yellow Pages.

3. Ask them for bids based on your plans.

4. Be friendly with your prospective builder but don't be a sheep dog. The French have an expression, "La confience n'ex-

clue pas le control." The Russians borrowed it, they pronounce it, "Do ver yai, no pro ver yai." During the Cold War, we used it: "Trust but verify." I do not like the expression. I still want to trust my instincts, but I should have verified Don's credentials.

5. Telephone 587-3295. R.I.C.O. Ask the operator if your contractor 1.) is licensed and 2.) if he has had any complaints against him and 3.) if there has been any legal action taken against him. If so, for what. Check, the complaints may not have been just.

6. A contractor's license may not be revoked unless he has one. A license is a reputation, a bond. If you sign a contract with an unlicensed contractor, the contract means nothing, he cannot readily be sued or fined. But you are not entirely safe even if you sign with a licensed one. All "homeowner builder" contracts can be dangerous. We are the ducks. No matter how little we may have we are still considered The Very Rich because we are building something. A few licensed contractors no matter how licensed they may be, are still out to pry whatever they can from us and make it look legitimate.

7. Study the bids from your three contractors. Study the contracts the spec sheets. If you are not qualified to do so, find someone who is. Make sure the fine points are covered down to the texture of the plastering. Paint, electrical outlets, clean-up, roofing materials, everything. You don't want any surprises. Some builders will write in the absolute minimum elements knowing that these may be discussed with the homeowner and that each change will be costly to him.

8. When you have narrowed your list down to one contractor, don't be too busy to pick up the telephone and call the references he lists. Don's first reference was a woman who had thrown him out. He owed her money. She opened up to me, a stranger. He had traumatized her twelve-year-old son, he had left her house in chaos with a year-long unfinished kitchen reno-

vation. She wanted to put it all behind her. This was Don's first reference. I never called the second.

9. When you are ready to sign the contract, as well as you can, make sure that the work is done in steps that match your installments. That there is no balloon payment up front, no meaningless "deposit upon acceptance." Enthusiasm can be blinding.

POST SCRIPTUM

In Babylonian times (4,000 BC) there were stronger building laws. The bricks a contractor used had to bear his personal cartouche so that if his roof fell in on you, you could track him down and have him put to death. Legally. Those were the days. I like the sound of that. Now we can only vandalize his van.

Forget about Don. He is a silverfish, the ancient household insect found in drains. Instead of being the salt of the earth, he turned out to be the carrion of the earth. There's a place for the morally bankrupt in our society just as there is a place for lousy weather or cockroaches or disease. The hyena cleans the veldt. With pleasure goes pain. Don has a place. He is unwanted but necessary to our balance. If all was too good we'd have to invent Don. What if everyone were honest? We need him if only to define our morality.

Anyway, my other news is good. My doctor told me last week that I have been given an extension. My option was picked up. Remission.

And I've found a new builder. An older ex-Navy man who works nearly always alone. Highly skilled, slow, honest. The minimum I ask. Maybe now after three months of standing in its underwear, the house *Hale ka'ao* will be dressed and painted and I'll start to make up for three months of lost work. This morning, I can't see why not.

DER WALDERGEIST

૭৽৽ৡ

The Twins: Their Rivalry went beyond life back before their birth into the womb where they clashed. And when they were born the babies were wonderfully opposite as if both sides of one divided brain had been joined into one.

It was 3:30 in the afternoon when Kurt came into the bedroom and drew the curtains wide. The late sun breaking through the forest burst into the room and flooded the brocaded walls. He removed the receiver from the telephone and held it over the sleeping man.

"Sir."

"Yes Kurt," the man spoke softly. Waking from his nap. He was not a young man and he woke slowly, re-entering the world with caution.

"It's the nurse on the telephone."

He took the receiver. Eric Carlsmann sat then and listened. After a moment he smiled. "I shall come to you." He handed the receiver to Kurt.

"Good news Sir?"

"Yes Kurt, I think it is very good news."

But it was not very good news. Twins had been born to him and twins had not been what he wanted, but twins were what he gotten. He'd wanted a single heir, not two. And he had not asked about their mother's condition. But they were boys and Carlsmann was delighted to have bred at all. And even though with the boys came a slight disappointment he knew that after all there might have been a girl born to him. His hopes that a single heir inherit his estate were dashed. Twins meant that the estate would need to be naturally divided. Wouldn't it? He did not know about such matters and that afternoon he called his jurist and studied a map of Wilderhafen but could find no decent way to break the forest, the meadows and the lake in half; especially the manor house. And so he decided his heir would be the first twin born. It was his last chance after all.

Carlsmann: Erlich Carlsmann had grown up with the twentieth century, and with the twenty-first century he knew that he was on his way out. His ancestral estate Wilderhafen had survived two centuries of wars and in the last one Carlsmann had been conscripted at sixteen and made a corporal in the first waffen infantry on the Russian front.

At Stalingrad he was one of the few who survived his horrors with his mind and body intact. Slightly wounded above the knee he walked with an attractive limp and carried a slim gleaming walking stick.

His father, a general, had acquired a good deal of fine art during the war and these paintings had come from disputed origins and were very, very good paintings. They had been stored in a vault beneath the stone floor of the chapel but that neither the Russians or the Americans had been able to discover.

After the general died Carlsmann had traveled the continents and so carried on as a roué in Paris, Venice, Buenos Aires, Rio de Janeiro, even in New York. Anywhere that was not Stalingrad. He would sell one painting surreptitiously then move on. He behaved as an illustrious figure and was attractive to women; but had never found one who could fill the far end of the long dining table in the Great Hall at Wilderhafen. Or fill the far end of his life, and when that last painting had been sold he dipped into his inheritance gambling on stocks and real estate on both Rivieras. But places he loved were evolving, becoming other places he did not know or care to know from Nice to Rio.

Some places like Mougins in the south of France had disappeared entirely under a freeway. They simple were not there anymore, and he always had Wilderhafen to come home to, and he frequently did. And he did not want it to become one of those renewed places. Or for it to progress in any way.

And so in a crowded time when cities and villages were changing helplessly before his eyes, Wilderhafen had not. It's miles of forested land were remote and withstood the upheavals of development, technology and architecture. It did not move into the future and so Eric Carlsmann had wanted it to remain.

Then one evening sitting by himself in a nearly deserted cinema, in Rome, his hair as sure as shoe polish his wounded leg unbent as he read the yellow sports pages and waited for the lights to go black he realized that time was not infinite. He was a man alone after all; he wanted a heir.

In Paris he made an arrangement with a suitable woman less than half his age from a good family in need of an income. He would have his heir. And now at Wilderhafen, graying while dressed in forty-five year old Saville Row suits, always an Hermés scarf dangling from the breast pocket gliding in a sort of Foxtrot across the stone floors of the rooms and terraces in ascot and velvet slippers he confined himself to growing roses and collecting stamps; he affected his excellent walking stick that he used more to smite the air thrashing at weeds than to support himself.

At Home: The day after they were born the twins were brought home to the manor house at Wilderhafen. The clouds which had amassed dark and purposely all morning long as though the day would storm, suddenly opened gaps between them. They broke apart as if they had been made of bone China and revealed a sky so blue, so deep, one could imagine going there and the day became fine, people noticed it. The midwinter gala of sun sparkling on the snow and the deep forest dressed in its embroidered white lace against the dark mystery beyond were a fine omen.

The twins were brought home, not to their mother, but to their governess Frau Ilona. Their mother had gone, she would live in Vienna; it had been arranged. The doctor had reported to Carlsmann that one of the twins in the womb had encroached on the other's space and had crowded his brother and they clashed and when it came time to be born it was the weaker twin who had been forced out first. The second born was the stronger. And from the first day at Wilderhafen Carlsmann was drawn to him. The one who'd shoved his smaller brother out of their mother's womb, and he was nearly two pounds heavier and more robust.

The doctor told Carlsmann that it was a miracle the small one had not been still born. That he had survived his ordeal and that when he first appeared under the premier lights it had been a mythic triumph. But it was he, the weaker, who became heir to Wilderhafen; it was a matter of the doctor's legal record entered in his journal that the smaller twin had been born a moment earlier than the strong one. But still, Carlsmann had named the second born after himself, Erlich. The other he had named Eric.

Rivalry and Favoritism: From their beginning Eric was less aggressive than Erlich. That was his charm. It was lost on his father who had survived Stalingrad and did not admire gentleness in men.

Erlich Carlsmann was an old man, his military eyes still bright under his lids folded into hoods. His cheeks fallen, his startling posture. The reformed Nazi corporal was contentedly at home without regrets. Proud of Wilderhafen and proud of his twin boys; but it seemed, prouder of Erlich. Erlich excelled in kindergarten, Eric did not. Erlich would become anything he wanted but with luck Eric would one day maybe become a poet or an artist a writer of serious books. But Eric had already become aggressive, ambitious, pushy, and he was described by Frau Ilona as hyper-kinetic. He built, climbed, inquired, destroyed and bullied. Eric was sweet and passive and introspective; he was whatever Eric wasn't, and it was as if together they formed one normal boy. When their governess quit, Mrs. Mapp came. When Mrs. Mapp left, Mademoiselle came; and when she left Miss Eden came; and when she left, Frau Ulag, whose grandmother had prepared meals in the kitchens of Auschwitz, came, took control and stayed on.

Others were uncomfortable around Erlich. Adults. He was too clever and too frank. He asked too many questions; but they still sensed that one day they would be paying attention to him.

The boys were similar in appearance but not identical. Eric was mild, even sweet, some said; and at an early age they could see that he would be passive. He did not do well in first and second grades; but spent his first year raising bugs and finding stray animals. Anything with a heart beat. He had a beautiful head of light-brown hair that fell into his eyes. The twins were mysterious, why wouldn't they be. They were two beings with one mind. And if they loved each other they did not show it, brothers don't. They were beyond trivial shows of affection. Eric and Erlich were children after all, not yet ten, and they were close; sometimes they were one boy. Once they reported the same nightmare at breakfast. Sometimes they were enemies, and when they fought it was Erlich who was the aggressor and the eventual winner. They fought like convicts. They were lifers after all. Living out their sentences. Eric could only defend himself and came to rely on biting to get out of his brother's head locks. Erlich won their fights, not because he was bigger, he wasn't much; he simply needed to win, and Eric did not. Eric did not consider winning of any special importance. And one morning when the boys were seven Frau Ulag found them locked in combat on the kitchen floor, each holding a knife; it was as though Erlich wanted Eric dead. Eric wanted other things that did not include constant battling with Erlich. He saw the lands around him; the estate that spread out over the dark valley the wooded ridges on either side. The forest, beyond the meadow, the deer, the squirrels, the foxes, the ravens the eagles and he wanted that world, the one he saw around him. To him it seemed to be a nation without borders that went on forever.

Erlich's ambitions lay elsewhere. Everyone agreed that he would become a success at whatever he decided to do with his life, and his father gave him whatever he wanted and entitled him to privileges, and Eric, who was not even allowed to own a dog, remained his heir.

Each twin had a turret room. To enter Erlich's was to enter a delightful space lab of electronic toys, science games, and computer paraphernalia. Eric needed nothing in his room except leaves and rocks and pieces of wood that he'd found on his walks. Things he thought were beautiful. On his walls were pictures of animals cut from magazines.

On their ninth birthday Calrsmann gave Erlich his grandfather's Iron Cross and he gave Eric a book of poems by Rainer Maria Rilke. Eric hugged his father sincerely. He believed he'd gotten the better present. Erlich just laughed.

Wilderhafen was so wide that no one crossed it. The boys had been warned about the forest. A giant lived there. He had escaped from the insane asylum at Neumark and roamed the woods and ate raw deer and wild boar. He also ate children, of course. And children had disappeared. There were red-eyed wolves. It was nonsense, but theses were the tales the boys were told.

The Discovery: And so on a radiant spring morning when Eric was nine he entered the forbidden forest. The first few steps he was not afraid, but when the cool darkness of the tall trees closed around him murmuring, he became terrified. The horizons were too close. But he walked on, and then it was alright.

The forest was waking up after a hard winter. Sun broke

through the high branches; butterflies bobbed in and out of the shadows. Birds announced his coming. The air was saturated with the rich odor of melting spring. Last autumn's leaves, over moist earth, of loam and decaying wood. The forest was not benign. It seemed to be moving round him, replacing itself. Growing in surges from fuses set deep in the bursting earth. He felt welcome; the forest beguiled him.

The Forest: a place that enclosed him in a world so deep that when he turned around to see where he had been he saw no path behind him; and there was none before him. And when he first entered he entered with disbelief. He was in a wondrous dark land; he was alone with the things and beings he loved. Often he would surprise deer. He knew nothing of the forest; it was the opposite of his life at the manor house. Here he was neither above or below anyone. He was one with the forest. He knew that this dark land would always enchant him, and he dreamt of becoming lost within its green ramparts, and unable to find his way out and having to live there. It was not a nightmare. It was a dream that came back to him again and again. He could never feel lost he was in a place he wanted to be. He was lost at home. He was not at home, at home. He felt the spirit of the forest. Der Waldergeist. There he felt older than he was; he felt at peace, and even though he was nine he knew that this is where he wanted to be for the rest of his life. He wanted nothing else away from the forest. He even imagined one day finding a little girl his age to come and live with him there. A small solitary figure walking deeper and deeper each day. The deer silent around him watching, unseen. The birds raucous overhead, sending out alarms throughout the high trees, and the boy walking into the forest smiling. As he passed between its green pillars, his wish was to grow in the forest as part of its trees. Der Waldergeist. The blood of the land. He entered with a feeling familiar to him. That he'd once slept and woken there. That he had once lived and died there. We are of the forest after all; we are not from the desert, or the sea.

Eric's forest was more than trees. He heard music, deep moaning sounds that haunted travelers, since there had been travelers. A place of watching eyes. A place of smells, a place of ferns and moss and plants and small white flowers at his feet. Of course there was no one to tell him their names. But why would he want to know their names. Knowing names is never part of knowing. And he would lie down and watch ants and beetles clean the swarming floor. It was ancient, and within it he felt eternal. And that like any great city, it would remain unknown to him forever.

Erlich had no interest in forests or squirrels or bugs or the tales that Eric brought him. His goal was a world of invention of computers, electronics, a world that was constantly replacing itself like the forest. Here was Erlich, his twin brother, ready for the world pointed in the direction of success, and here was Eric surrounded by trees. Was he retarded? He could have been, but he had found his destination. As if he were running away to sea or running away to join the circus. And running away is always part running from, and part running to. And though he always came home in the afternoon at tea-time and slept in his own bed at night, Wilderhafen was never so much his home as the forest was. It was the perfect discovery. It lured him in. He told Frau Bauer, the cook, of his secret excursions and the two maids, but not Kurt, the butler, or Frau Ulag. If Frau Ulag knew she would smack him severely and report him to his father, who would put him under house arrest.

Whenever he went into the forest he would take a loaf of bread from the kitchen and a thermos of tea and wrap, in a napkin, jam, or bratwurst sandwiches, and all the while, as he was walking in, he would feed the birds and the squirrels and the rabbits. An invisible deer followed him at a distance.

The Grove: He walked deeper in each day entering with fresh

intensity. Now a mile from the manor house he came across a grove of trees noticeably different from the pines and the others around it; toward the center of the grove stood a lone tree more beautifully formed than the others. Magnificent beyond any tree he'd seen. It stretched its great black arms as if waking from a deep sleep; and it reached wide on all sides shouldering its way above the others to lure the hawks and the eagles, who flew high in the forest. Clearly this tree was its patriarch. It attracted Eric like a forbidden rule. The tree was dead. He could not imagine for how long because no one buries a tree after it dies. The brutal years had hollowed out its trunk. And he was quick to see an opening the size of a small door at the base of its trunk and he saw another opening above the first branches and from there he found he could enter the trunk and slide down inside its hollowed heart and there was just enough room at the bottom for him to squat, open his napkin, eat what he had brought, drink his tea, then, when he was finished, leave by the natural doorway. In the time he was inside the tree he felt a rapture, as if he were part of this great tree, that he had grown inside it, that it was the only place for him to be in the world. His domain, not his brother's, or father's. Not anyone's. His. His own Wilderhafen. All summer long, and in the winter.

And then he was ten.

One bleak, icy day, Erlich, secretly followed Eric. The forest was taking its mid-winter nap. The trees asleep, the rabbits and foxes gone to ground; there was no odor. The black boughs were silent; snow covered the ground. The light was dimming by the time Eric got to the tree; snow whiskered its great black arms. Its hundred fingers reached out to the forest on all sides. As he was climbing to the lower branches he spotted Erlich standing off half hidden by a tree in the snowy clearing. How out of place his brother looked. How little he knew of where he was, or what Eric knew. He glanced down at his brother and for the first time in his life he pitied him, standing off alone, out of place in the forest. Eric, was a waldergeist, after all.

He turned away and skillfully entered the tree from above and was gone from sight. Maybe it was bravado, maybe he was showing off, but Eric forgot he was carrying in the pockets of his jacket, his thermos of tea and his sandwiches, and so he did not slide very far down the inside of the trunk. Midway he stopped and the tree held him wedged by his own weight, his arms useless. He was hopelessly stuck in the chute inside the great tree.

Erlich assumed his brother would appear at the opening below. A minute went by and then another, finally he called. "Eric?" Did he hear a muffled sound coming from the tree? He wasn't sure. Then he knew. He'd heard that chimney sweeps used little boys because they were small enough to squeeze down chimneys, but every so often one would become inextricably lodged and died. No sound had come from the tree. He called again. "Eric?" As if to confirm what was already clear. He heard nothing. He became frightened. He stood frozen. Unable to move toward the tree, unable to run for help. His feet were cold; he simply stood transfixed. He stared at the tree waiting for it to issue his brother. But it did not.

Love between twins can be the most elaborately pure love that two souls can possibly feel in this world. Or there can be the wildest hatred and the wickedest jealousy. There is no logic among these feelings because a twin feels about his other self, the way he feels about himself, and so is capable of showing no mercy to him. Erlich's face was burning with cold and he called "Eric" and he did not call again. And if he heard the tree answer the sound died somewhere deep inside him. And he took a step backwards hardly knowing what he was doing. It was a raw day. No sense loitering about the forest. He took another step backward staring at the tree.

So many reach their ultimate goal by committing a single

grievous sin. One, no more, grievous single sin is self forgiving and Erlich backed away from the tree step by step, his mind numb; you can do so much by not doing anything.

Erlich backed away. As he did he might have heard sounds emanating from the tree, small animal sounds; he turned and ran; the sounds grew smaller and smaller. Each time he stopped to catch his breath and he imagined he heard them until finally they were gone and the forest was silent. He kept running and at Wilderhafen he burst into the dining room ignoring the guests and went to his father in tears.

"Father, Eric has drowned in the leben fluss above the falls." And he described what had happened on the cracked ice at the frozen lake. Not at the tree, but near to the outlet where the icy water rushes to the falls above a fast moving stream swollen by melting snow above. Frau Ulag was fired on the spot.

"Poor little Eric," Kurt whispered to the staff in the kitchen. He has gone down the falls and is already in the Danube by now, going to the sea.

The cook burst into tears. The maids cried openly. Eric had been the staff's favorite and they had shared his love of the forest with him. But he was gone.

Eighteen years later. Erlich was 28 and quite successful when he found his bride. She was lovely and she was strong, and unlike him, she'd come from a hard working family with an ambitious honest father who had clawed his way to the top of a difficult profession. Her name was Monika Sachs and she did everything thing with great ease, from building a fire, to building a goat house. From sewing clothes, to baking bread, to scouring pots and pans, no work was inconvenient. Carlsmann, who had been bedridden, was now much better, up and walking around the property overjoyed. Not only did he have an heir, but he would be having grandchildren to carry on his tradition at Wilderhafen. The date was set for late spring and as a wedding present he would build a smaller version of the manor house, a replica, set across the meadow from Wilderhafen a quarter mile away. Much the same as Louis XIV built the Petite Trianon to stand off away from Versailles. It was the perfect gift, and he filled the house with furniture that Monika and Erlich had picked out, but the dining room required a long table and that could not be found at any store. So Carlsmann sent the loggers into the forest to find a suitable tree for carpenter to make one. After two days of walking the loggers came across a grove of black trees a mile from the manor house. And a great dead tree stood at its center. They felled it and milled it on the spot into six-meter lengths and then dragged them out of the forest by a team of oxen. They did not recognize the wood; they had never seen it before. Black and dense, the most un-yielding they had come across. A carpenter recognized it as European black walnut, a tree thought to be long extinct, and he was right.

Carlsmann found among the estate's papers that in the 1700s seeds for the trees had come from Estonia and had been planted by Baron Carlsmann, a deranged ancestor, who had it in his lunatic brain that the French were trying to kill him. And so he planted dozens of these trees believing that they owned magical powers and he could hide from his pursuers. Years after the Baron had been gently led away from his estate to more suitable quarters, the black walnut trees had grown to maturity, been forgotten, and discovered. Some had died. But the rest had been allowed to grow for two centuries forming their grove hidden deep within the forest.

The black table was massive. Its weigh required half-a-dozen sets of legs, each of which was nicely turned. It was not a wide table but it was more than five-meters long. A magnificent table; but the carpenter noticed a sticky substance that could not be cleaned emanating from the table top covering a small section at one end. He told Erlich that the tree was sapping.

"How could sap come from wood so long dead?"

"Not unheard of," the carpenter told him "for dead wood to continue excreting sap. It would be similar to a corpse growing hair and fingernails in the grave."

Erlich didn't mention the emanating sap to his father; the table was a gift after all; and the wood was such a rarity. There were no more European black walnut trees left anywhere on earth. He let it be.

Erlich's Wedding: An extravagance of guests filled every bed in both manor houses. Gifts were piled everywhere. On the eve of his wedding Erlich sat at the head of his new table. The Thane. And throughout the evening many toasts had been drunk to each others health. It was now late. Erlich banged his chalice down hard on the table top. The candles were down. The servants had been dismissed for the night. A cooling buffet lined the wall. Decanters of wine and lager were passed along the table. There was schnapps.

Erlich touched the table top with his fingers as he talked. Under his fingers tips he felt the sap. He let the candle before him flicker in his gaze, nearly hypnotizing him; nothing mattered that night. He was at home at Wilderhafen and it was all his. He wiped his fingers, then touched whatever it was in the sticky texture again. He moved the candle closer to him to better see what it was. There seemed to be fibers, maybe a few strands, nothing more. While he listened to conversations he scratched at the fibers with his fingernail trying to free them, but he couldn't. The sap was sticky and he poured wine on his fingertips again and wiped them on his napkin. But as he watched his guests his fingers went back to whatever was emanating from the table top. It wasn't fiber but whatever it was he could not free it from the wood. One final toast. The guest divided and went into various rooms and to bed. The candles burned down. Erlich kissed his bride goodnight. They went to separate rooms and fell down hard on his bed and he passed out without removing his clothes. But in an hour he was awake and wondering why. The house, the guests asleep, his bride asleep. Silence. And he came downstairs.

The table was in disarray. Wine spilled; broken china; forks; hardening pudding; open game birds; wine stained napkins. Two guttering candles on the candelabra stood at his end of the empty table. And he sat at his place and stared down its length. Alone in the dining room. What had brought him back? The fibers, there they were flattened into the table surface; he had not imagined them. There seemed to be more of them. He drew the candelabra over to him; he could see the fibers formed a pattern. He touched some strands, isolated a few, but they were too fine, to fine to be fiber. They were hair. Hair. As he stared the surface of the table seemed to dissolve slightly. It seemed to liquify. The table top became a black pool, dense.

Erlich glimpsed for an instant at the great tree in the dead of winter as it was that final time when he backed away from it. Heat seared his body and he suddenly felt sick. Something was forming on the surface. The hair became a lighter color, wavy, as if it had been combed. Then he saw it. A profile of a head forming a detail, the head of a child. Eric, his sweet face seen from the side as if he was a bas relief sculpture struck on a coin. His nose, his cheek, his eye, his beautiful hair emerging. Emerging, from the depth of the black walnut table top. Eric was emerging swimming in the dark wood of the table as if he'd become part of the tree and the tree was now finally giving him up a waldergeist made eternal by the tree; his other self coming back to his twin from the heart of the tree.

The morning was dark the first person in the dining room was the chauffeur passing through to the kitchen. He'd been visiting one of the maids and had stopped by the dining room in search of some scraps, venison or pheasant, to take with him for breakfast. Maybe some lager. The room was dim. He saw a form spread across the massive black table top and assumed it was a sleeping guest.

The chauffeur passed out when he recognized his employer; he was obviously dead, his mouth open wide in a scream. His fingers were buried in the table top as if the wood had allowed his fingers to enter it and then had closed around them. Carlsmann's physician, his lifelong friend, Willy Silverling examined Erlich that morning. His heart had simply stopped, he told him; a stroke probably brought on by extreme alcohol and excitement. He covered the body with a blanket and refused to discuss how his fingers had been able to reach inside the table top. He advised Carlsmann that no other doctor should see Erlich and that nothing should be said about his death. Further, Silverling could not remove Erlich's fingers from the wood, and refused to sever them surgically. Erlich was buried the next day with his hands joined to a fragment of the black walnut tabletop. It was no ordinary wood after all, known to be the most unyielding on the continent.

AUGUST 11

As usual, I do most of the talking. I want to meet him away from the house, so I catch up with him downtown. The Woman isn't feeling so hot today. Anyhow, she's not even his mother. So. We come down to this waterfront bar where we can look across the Admiralty Inlet at the islands. But there's fog.

It's his twenty-first birthday, August the eleventh. That's the only day I get to see him. Not that we don't get along, he just isn't around very much. But I can always nail him down for his birthday. He keeps that day open for me.

This bar is called The Ship. No mystery there; there's every ship model you want: clipper ship, tanker, destroyer, galleon, sloop. We stand up against the bar. He doesn't talk, just stares at the ship models.

He isn't the drinker I am by any means, not many are. Don't think I have a problem, I don't. But because August eleventh falls on a Saturday this year, I don't have any compunctions about drinking this early in the day. I don't ever drink much at home; I mean I could and I do, but I need to keep an eye on the Woman, who is Evelyn, who makes me listen to her vacuum cleaner, smell her God-damned Murphy's Oil.

Now we're standing over at the plate glass window. As I say, there's fog out there this morning; it's too foggy to see the San Juan Islands across the inlet.

Josh stands straight, straighter than me, and he's every bit as tall, and where a couple of my fingernails are black or busted, his are clean and straight. Plus he has all ten of his fingers. I have eight. Where my skin is kind of mottled, his is smooth. Where my hair ends, his begins. He has my nose, I guess, a smaller version of it, and his mother's eyes. She's long dead, of course, but I can see her in his face. His dead mother.

He stands at the big plate-glass window looking out into the fog, away from me, toward Vancouver Island. I can see his eyes in the glass. He never once starts our conversations. He never looks directly at me; he tends always to look away. But if he ever did look at me, like he did once last birthday, I'd see doubt in his eyes as if he's pissed off at me.

See, Josh thinks for himself; I never told him what to think; he's not handed his opinions. He says you can't wait around for luck to happen to you; you gotta kick luck in the butt and tell her what time to show for work. I like that. He wants to build his own company, six employees. Something to do with wood. Anything, he loves wood. To quote him exactly, he wouldn't work for a boss, only for a dream. I guess it's pretty clear I love the boy.

Me? I was always told what to think. Twenty years in the navy, a half-inch stripe, and then construction work, still taking orders. Then the accident. So let's be honest here, I've been fighting my way to the bottom, driving down the center lane on the Road to Nowhere, looking for the crock at the end of the rainbow. The crock of shit. Face it, we're all lifers.

Tonight I've decided I'm bringing Josh home to supper, no matter what the Woman says. What the hell, it's his twenty-first August eleven.

The Woman and me, there's a natural pair. What's the opposite of love at first sight? Religious woman, she can see the bad in everything. Sex never came naturally to Evelyn; it was one of her household jobs. She has so few new thoughts, she's dangerous. Don't look for anything you can't find and you won't be disappointed, she tells me. She buys with coupons. Buys nothing she can't scrub. She cleans. I tell her too much cleaning kills life. There're men go for women who don't want them to be the way they are, and I guess you marry the first woman who figures you out before you do. So, I've been married to a dead woman who is very alert to my list of my personal habits, some of which have always given her pain, drinking and cigars to name two. Josh is included on that list.

Heads turn when we walk into a bar, me talking to Josh about whatever I want. Bartenders eye us coolly; the drinkers watch us. I guess we look like we could rearrange the decor if we felt like it. Josh is not macho; I never raised him to be. But if you don't have perfect manners, a little physical strength is essential.

We've been having an plain old fashioned birthday party today. We know how to drink without hurting ourselves. We were asked very politely to leave The Ship this afternoon. So we left. We walked over to this other bar. Very dark, like a Swiss tavern, where the bartender suggested after a couple of drinks that we leave because, he said, I got to laughing too loud. Laughing too loud? Excuse me? But he suggested it politely.

So here we are. Strolling along this sidewalk. No more fog, it's a clear night. I'm walking perfectly straight. Meticulously, in fact. Trying to locate a telephone, so we go in this bar called The Inside Track. Stirrups, photos of dead jockeys. I'm calling home trying to determine what we will be dining on tonight and if there might be enough food for a third mouth.

"Where are you?" the Woman says.

"I'm here."

"Where?"

"Never been here before. They got a horse's head on the wall it's got a glass eye looking right at me." I'm talking very carefully, clipping my words, making sure she can grasp what I'm saying. All with an idea to bring Josh to the table.

"Dinner was at six-thirty, John; she hits the was like she was talking to a retard. It's all put away, now."

"Don't you know what day this is?"

She doesn't say anything.

"I'm with Josh."

Evelyn always turns sour when I mention Josh.

"Please come home, John," she says quietly.

"Not. Without. Josh." I say this as deliberately as I can, so she'll understand it. She doesn't say anything for a couple of seconds.

"Where exactly are you?"

I tell her where exactly I am: The Inside Track.

She doesn't have a clue where that one is.

"John, please."

I tell her I'm not 100% sure where I parked the car.

"We'll find it tomorrow," she says. "Take a taxi."

It's never been easy to talk to the Woman about Josh; she just can't seem to grasp that about him.

There is no taxi. It's a good two-mile walk home but the weather's cleared.

On this black night, walking away from the lit streets, the stars touch the face of the land. I tell Josh, You can touch those stars, Josh, never mind how. I know I can. You can touch any one of them. Tell me what star you can't touch, Josh. You can touch any thing.

Now I'm standing with him at the front door. I press the buzzer. Even under the door I can smell her goddamn Murphy's Oil; she's waxed the floors again.

I whisper to him, "You'd better stand over there, out of the line of fire." I know what Evelyn is going to say. Josh moves into the shadows. I press the buzzer harder.

Here she comes, clip clop clip clop across her waxed floor. The Woman's heels sound like horseshoes. When she opens the door, I swear, she's going to be wearing her best poker-face.

I know she's going to tell me that Josh never was. I know she's going to say he was aborted, that this is the anniversary of his abortion, August eleven, twenty-one years ago. I know she's going to say that, I know it.

Gardner McKay

THE MALOCCHIO PEARLS

When B.L. got home, into the living room, the old woman was sitting in the rocking chair eyes closed, motionless. Through the window, the sun was low behind her, lying just above the rigs of the fishing boats which were all named after hopes, in the harbor below.

The old woman slept so still. Right away B.L. wondered as he always did coming home, Is she dead?

She'd always slept in the late afternoon but so far had always woken up. Anyway, most of the time, May Breadstone seemed on the verge of dying, more like quitting, her heart broken as it had been, she had told B.L. more than a few times, by her fiancé so many many years before and her heart had never properly healed. His name had been Turpin and they were to be married at Christmas forty-two years ago, the winter he had shipped out of Boston on the Esso tanker Franklin and had never turned home again; he had simply disappeared into the sea, sailed away and abandoned the young woman. He had written a last letter telling her to look out to the horizon on some evenings because that was where they would meet again. She had been doing just that for forty-two years.

This afternoon B.L. noticed the old woman looked different, but he couldn't tell what it was. She was wearing what she always wore, work dress with pinky-brown cotton stockings to where you could see them rolled to her knees, not above. Work shoes. Her hair in fragments. She kept herself looking pretty miserable. Just in case he were to get any filthy ideas. He was the hired. As the hired he was never meant to rise to her level. It was understood by both of them that she represented his betters. That to

45

have opinions you needed to own property. And there were other differences.

Looking at May Bredstone's face B.L. caught the wet glint of her eyes. She's not dead. He now saw what was different about her this evening; it was an expression; she was sleeping with an expression on her face. The expression was one of peace and calm.

She was a small woman with pointed nose and eyes who never went out of her way to spread any joy in the world as far as B.L. could see, and here she was sleeping with the trace of a smile on her face.

Well, think you o' that, he said to himself.

B.L.'d gotten used to answering the old woman's first question when he walked into the house at the end of every one of his days, salt-stuck from his jobs on the docks or the fishing boats. She'd always have a small chore ready for him, something that had fallen apart during the course of the day, and if nothing had, she'd make something up.

Just so long as B.L. remembered his place, as if every day, the old woman needed to reaffirm hers. A dozen or so years ago she'd just about let him have her basement room with the small too-high window to live in, and he paid almost no rent. For that, he kept the pipes clear, the steps nailed, the house painted, the rugs beaten, the drains working, the roof mended, the yard raked and so on.

Just everything but bark at strangers, she'd told him when he took the room.

B.L.'s arms were garnished with tattoos, some of them gone bad, shady names, rotten flowers. He drank poor whiskey, stuff that hurt going down. His vocabulary was small and too raw for May Breadstone to tolerate at the dining table, and so in spite of their closeness within the walls of the small two-storey house, they ate together only on Sundays.

Anyone who tattoos ladies' names on his arms can't have a good mind. she thought. He's just a coarse little boy who's forty or so and claims he dreams of owning his own fishing boat.

Tilliantown was a plain 18th century fishing village on the Maine coast two hundred sea miles north of Boston and despite the business world's need to overrun it still resembled a fishing village as it had around 1900 with the same population it had then.

B.L. stood facing her. Outside the living room, the small harbor sparkled between the trees below the house; he watched two fishing boats coming home, their nets high, drying.

He stood; he waited for the old woman to wake up; he listened for her breathing. Tired of waiting, he turned back and closed the door again loudly. Her mouth opened as she woke, then her eyes. She wondered where she was; she had been gone a long way off and back in time. She wiped her mouth.

"You been sleeping, Missus May?"

"'Course I been sleepin'. What'dja think I was doin'?"

"What job do you need attended to tonight, Missus May?"

"Why nothing, B.L., I don't need nothin. What time have you got there?"

He took out his pocket watch. "Be close to six thirty."

"My, my, my." She touched her neck.

Then he saw it.

A strand of pearls hung from her neck. When she touched them he had seen them. She never wore jewelry; why should she wear it? She was poor. And who'd she wear it for even if she owned it? Now the sunlight came from the window behind her. He could not see the strand of pearls well, but they shone hot and dark like young flesh against her ruined skin.

"What's that you got around your neck, Missus May? You wearin' jewels."

"That's right, B.L. these are pearls."

She touched the necklace again, sighed, and smiled.

"Pearls?"

She gave him the most radiant smile he had ever seen her give anyone.

"I didn't know you had any pearls."

"I didn't neither, but I had 'em a long time."

"How do you mean that?"

"How old are you, B.L.?"

"You know that."

"Well, I might of had 'em since just about the time you were born."

"I thought you was supposed to be so poor."

For an instant a slight air of superiority passed across her face; she lifted her chin to him then she laughed.

"Well, that's just what I'm telling you, B.L.; I didn't know that I had 'em 'til this afternoon."

"Well, where in hell'd they come to you from?"

"Don't curse, B.L., no need for that. I was given them by Mitchell."

It was Mitchell Turpin who had destroyed her this long long time ago. Mitchell Turpin who had shipped out of Boston on an oil tanker, and she was never married to him but promised, when he disappeared.

"Dead Mitchell Turpin give 'em to you?"

B.L. could be so coarse. "My Mitchell gave 'em to me."

"Come on, Missus May. He couldn't give 'em to you, he's been gone forty years."

"They're from him, B.L. I found 'em hidden 'em in that footstool. He left 'em for me."

B.L. saw the footstool, nodded. It had been ripped apart, stuffing laid aside, the new bought fabric still folded, brass-headed tacks scattered on the rug. An empty flat box on the floor, the name Airship Cigars written on it.

"They real?"

She nodded. "Oh, my, yes."

"They don't look too healthy to me."

"'Cause that's how dull they get when they've been let be too long." She took the strand from her neck and weighed it in her hands.

"How'd you know they're even real?"

"Anyone could see they're real."

"Can I hold 'em?" B.L. reached his hand out as if to take them.

May pulled the strand to her, dropped it back over her neck. The effect was magical. She became radiant.

"Whyn'n't you polish 'em up?"

"Maybe I will tomorrow." She lifted the strand of pearls like Josephine lifted her crown, on her fingers over her head; she wiped three or four, held them up so that the late sunlight caught them. The effect was amazing, the pearls came to life; a golden blue-pink haze rose out from them. He guessed there must be thirty-five of them, maybe more; the biggest of the lot being half-an-inch across.

"Whatever makes those pearls seem alive?" B.L. said. Even B.L. could see they were real.

"Must be worth hundreds, Missus May."

"I can only guess that these pearls be worth more than either one of us has ever laid eyes on."

Now the sun was setting. The excitement in her voice had turned to weariness. May Breadstone had nothing. She had always lived with nothing and with no hope for anything. Except for that one time.

"Let me see it."

She hesitated, now he was aware of her tears. He stared at her too long.

Later that night after B.L. had gone down the cellar stairs into his room and locked the door, May went over the glorious afternoon in her mind once again. It was a luxury to remember it.

The footstool had been her mother's. After years May had finally got around to sewing a new cover for it. The damask had been worn through for a long time; the rich blue had paled, there was black frayed along its edges; webbed threads were visible. When it was all off, the stuffing on the floor, the footstool stripped bare, she had seen the cigar box. Airship Cigars? The shock of it; she hadn't seen a box of those for decades. Airship Cigars had been Mitchell's favorite smoke. There was a Christmas card to her written in his dreadful big handwriting. Dizziness had overcome her. I love you, May.

When she'd opened the box she'd seen the pearls coiled there where they lay since he'd closed the box and stuffed it into the footstool. He had not abandoned her. He had always meant to come back to her.

She had lapsed away, then, moaning, folded into the rocking chair. She was grieving for him, not the way she had grieved when she was young and her grieving was vigorous. Now she grieved weakly, dying, all her tides were out. Grieving for Mitchell Turpin with a great sigh, for lost years when she might have learned everything there was to know about him. And him about her.

Holding the strand of pearls in one hand and the forty-two

year old greeting card in the other, she grieved that night as if she were ready to go find him on the horizon. She was an old woman, after all; everything was crucial. Nothing was crucial.

She held the pale brittle Christmas card closed. It was more than a Christmas card; it was a love letter. She could not make out every word he had written; Mitchell wrote in a firm vertical scrawl. On the back he wrote something that struck her as odd. In his huge scrawl, underlining every few words, he told her that the pearls were from Malay, they must always stay with her, must never be sold given or stolen. They were temple pearls, he wrote. She held the Christmas card. One word he spelled in block letters; malocchio. He used it twice. A feeling hovered over the word, akin to danger. She imagined things, maybe he had not bought them, maybe someone had died.

She felt so upset about the word that she called Vincente the grocer who was Italian. He said right away that the word malocchio meant cursed.

Now it was late, May's weariness was giving way to sadness, and she began to cry again quietly.

In Mitchell's huge scrawl, she read May please never ever sell these pearls. They're only for you to wear, you and only you. There's "malocchio" attached to them. This same old juker told me that in Singapore so I'm just passing the pearls on to you for safe keeping. But whether or not you believe in this wanga, that's what they call a curse, I'd always want you to be on the safe side.

When Mitchell came back from Singapore that last trip he must have brought the pearls; he hid them in the footstool, set aside for their wedding Christmas. Then he sailed. That's all she knew.

And he had not abandoned her. It was as if he knew he was going to die at sea.

B.L. had frightened her when he had reached out for them. He had stared at her too long. Her fear had passed in an instant, but she realized that B.L. had never owned anything of value in his lifetime. He could barely hold a job on the docks, or maybe on a fishing boat, a job that only required a man to have a strong stomach and good hands. Even light-headed from the night before B.L. was good for a day's work; he could always put out in all weather to raise the pots or haul in the nets or fishlines, hand over hand, according to the seasons on a fishing boats.

B.L. stared at May, thinking. The sallow photographs stood on the table behind her. Pictures of dead people. Her past, there was no present left to her, so little stood between her and her photographs.

There was nothing very surprising about B.L.'s call to Doctor Grant the next morning. He told him to get right over to the house. May had fallen down the back stairs and might be dead. She was an old woman and old women fell down and died easily. She had owned nothing of value. Whatever furnishings she left in her house went to the Seaman's Fund and the house itself went back to the county and there was no mention made of the twenty-two inch strand of flawless South Sea pearls that was probably worth more than B.L. could imagine. And even though he was given permission to stay on in the house as caretaker until the state made arrangements to sell it, he surprised them by saying No. The next day he took the train down to Boston to look at fishing boats.

He named her The Pearl. She was heavy and sound of hull, a good a high bow, lapstrake topsides, a marine diesel, a couple of bunks below. She was young, she'd been built in Narragansett Bay ten years before. The price of the pearls was far more than the price of a fishing boat, it was price of a new life. B.L. said it to himself, One life for another.

The night was so calm he could count the stars on the water and when B.L. held his hand up to the sky, he covered a hundred of them. The moon was so full so high so clear, he could describe the details of her wounds. She looked as if the galaxy had thrown rocks at her which of course it had been doing for quite some time. It was a moon under which he could see the mooring lines he was looking for. He switched off his riding lights, let go his lines and pushed off the dock.

The stars crowded the black surface ahead of his cleaving bow. When he was 'way clear of the land, several miles out, he cut his motor and let The Pearl glide. She had the weight to carry her a long way slowing, slowing, and finally after another quarter mile or so she drew to a standstill dead in the water. The stars surrounded B.L. from his shoulders upward; he could not remember a night as still as this night. And it was his.

Stillness. He dropped his navy anchor with a splash, he switched the riding lights on for safety and settled in to wait for the dawn aboard his own boat, his own first night at sea. The imperfect pearl moon was bright enough for him to sit on the taffrail and bait fishlines for the sunrise. When he had finished sorting his lines, baiting his hooks and setting his lures aside, he would go below and lie on his side in his bunk until he woke. Then he would make coffee in his own pot on his propane stove; he would eat the sweet Boston pastries he had stowed.

Without a jolt or a shiver, he was wet, swimming, water surrounding him. It was as if he had awakened in the water.

Had he fallen asleep on deck? He must have. There had been no splash, he was simply in the water, soaked, swimming. He looked around for his boat. It couldn't be far away.

He could not see it. He turned in circles splashing the water, scanning the still water. He ought to be able to see riding lights for miles, but there were no riding lights. The Pearl simply was not there. And it had not sunk. If it had the water would not be so calm.

He wore his sea-boots, his legs churning, his eyes inches free of the surface; he could no longer see the shore lights of Tilliantown, or know in what direction they lay.

He was surrounded by the night. He was out among the stars. Where the hell is my boat? There was no boat; his boat was gone as if it had never been. He knew that he was miles offshore, but he didn't know from which direction. The roaring din, his ears full of organ music, all stops pulled out. B.L. now knew he would drown. He had wondered about this moment, hundreds of times, close to positive it would come, never sure of course, but prepared for the worst. It was a solemn moment. B.L.'s sea boots were pulling him down.

The Pearl had vanished. How could he have been abandoned? Nothing was making sense to him. He couldn't understand how his boat had vanished. Gone as if it had never been.

He couldn't come to terms with his own drowning and he suddenly panicked; insanely confused he thrashed the water wildly crying out to the stars sobbing for his life, knowing all the time that nothing would change, that no one would save him, nothing he couldn't see was coming to rescue him. He opened his mouth and yelled, Oh Missus May, I'm sorry Missus May! I'm sorry. His mouth filled with sea water. The feeling of hopelessness, resignation. He had always wondered about this moment. How he would die. Now it was clear; it would not be in bed; there would be no tubes, no nurses, no welfare, medical aid, no disease, no last words, no old age.

He burned through his strength too quickly. When it drained from his legs and he slid under, below the surface, he pulled himself up with his arms thrashing like a rooster and when his arms gave up he slipped under, rose again in a convulsion, his brain still running after the body had quit. No more commands were being obeyed. He slipped away this time for good.

Below the surface, his legs worthless, his arms dead, as he descended he turned on his back, staring up; he glimpsed the moon for the last time, a wide shaky oval smeared out above him on the surface above him as he gently sank closer and closer to the bottom.

His eyes were wide open. Now he could see a slight glint standing in the water above him, between him and the moon. It was not a fish. It wasn't standing still, it was was dropping toward him.

His breath had gone. His lungs seared, they had burst. There was only delirium left, the final vestige of consciousness, the final giving.

Then he saw it. Free below the surface. The string of pearls was sinking slowly toward him. There it was above him. He grabbed at it. Too far. Just out of his reach. Suspended in the water, unclasped, barely descending with him. A sleeping snake.

As it passed him, B.L. he snatched for it once more, his fingers bent into a claw. He snagged it. As he did it whirled itself around his wrist and clasped itself.

Even at that moment he felt a glimmer of understanding, as if he had been dealt a fair blow. In that last instant, as he dreamed away his life, drowning, he knew; the fishing boat had returned into the string of pearls.

A Nantucket beach in the first light, a calm morning, before the gulls, a boy trotting alone sees a shape ahead of him partly buried in the wet sand. It is B.L., curled on his side, washed just above the small rill of sliding water.

A string of pearls has been wound tightly around his wrist, the clasp is shut. The pearls in the sunlight are more radiant than ever. To the boy they look as though they are being carried the way someone carries a priceless thing, by someone who is late for an appointment, someone who wants to do his duty and deliver the pearls safely to their destination.

THE IMPROMPTUS

You've heard of what happened in Pennington. Of course you have. You've heard of the Impromptus.

My name is Josh Marlowe. I'm a syndicated reporter at the New York Post, you've seen my name. I came here on deadline to Pennington after it happened. We all came to Pennington. Wasn't it a great story? A hell of a story, the reporter's dream. A positive story with cynical undertones involving teenagers. The Impromptus.

Those Minnesota kids are heroes. My kind, your kind, the best kind. National heroes. The kind who save lives in the community without regard to their personal safety. You've might have taken inspiration from my articles. How one gang of students stop one more high school massacre. Littleton, Paducah, Jonesboro, Pearl, Springfield, San Diego. Well subtract Pennington from that list. It would have been bigger than all of them combined. Not just one more sickening tragic riddle, but the world record high school massacre, which is what it's all about.

Which one of the Black Hand gang members confessed later that they were going for The Guinness Book of Records?

If it hadn't been for the Impromptus. Well, let's not dwell on that. This massacre was well-planned as any Israeli commando raid. The Black Hand gang's standing onstage for the Christmas Play the morning of December 18th. Their automatic weapons trained at the audience ready to open fire on the audience. Which happened to be the entire student body of Captain Grover High School plus its faculty members. 412 had all gathered waiting to see the Christmas Play; it was compulsory, and it came within seconds of happening.

Well, it's just a great story. Under my front page three-word headline:

TEENS SAVE SCHOOL

Amazing story wasn't it? Under that my byline, Josh Marlowe, maybe you've seen it. My lead sentence ran, "Hello America there's still hope for our kids. That we have such teenagers in our midst. That there are Impromptus present in our school system gives us all hope. Maybe that's what it's all about. Good versus evil. The Black Hands on one side of the chain link fence and The Impromptus on the other. And those kids are only 14, 15, 16, 17 years old." That's how I write, simple, direct. I believe in simplicity. Somehow they skipped me again this year for the Nobel Prize in Literature, maybe next year.

The Governor of Minnesota drove up here to Pennington, made a rousing speech and gave them all medals.

I stayed on after the governor went back to St. Paul. Nearly all of the reporters had left after that. The story was over.

Then that weekend the president invited them to the White House to give them presidential medals and I stayed on here. The silence in Pennington was eerie, me being from New York, but God I suddenly loved a good town square. Town hall at one end, churches of various persuasions at the other, and in between the good solid houses built in the 1800s by the town's founders. Everything in order. Dead quiet at night. It made me want to get out of New York and back to my roots if I'd had any, but I don't, coming from the city. My wife had wanted to fly in and join me. She was having a birthday. She was also having the flu. But still I stayed on here after the kids got back from Washington. I couldn't get enough of it. I couldn't leave. I liked the town, Pennington. But there was something else. It was too perfect.

I made an appointment to interview the mayor. I expected to meet a man, a politician in an LL Bean shirt smoking a pipe with a gun rack on his office wall, but aside from being a woman she didn't disappoint me at all; in her other life she's a history and biology teacher, a basketball and baseball coach. She asked me why I was staying on; I told her something odd had struck me about all of this. She asked what but I told her I didn't know, I just had this odd feeling about it. And by then all the reporters had left.

You see the thing that distinguishes the Impromptus from any other gang I ever heard of is that they have a penchant for wearing off-white linen suits and Panama hats. The Black Hands were your generic rebels in their black shirts, neo-Nazi. But the Impromptus look like characters out of a Noel Coward play. And they are different, the Impromptus, not because they wear those damn suits they keep to themselves. One might even call them snobbish. All the teenagers I've seen are all working hard to be different, but they all look alike to me. And they're afraid to be really different because they'll be laughed at, so they wear hoop and studs and tattoos and prison clothes with obvious labels and they all look the same to me. But the Impromptus look like American tourists in Cuba in the 1930s. Some wear flowers in their lapels, smoke with cigarette holders. They drink gin Martini's instead of smoking grass. They don't use cell phones; they hate computers. They all have high IQs. They meet every Wednesday afternoon in a rented garage. No one outside the Impromptus has ever been invited to see its interior. They are private; they are affected, exclusive and snobbish. They play chess. It is a secret society after all and teenagers want a secret life. But these are intellectual outcasts, and they're very bored by what they see around them.

When the kids came back from Washington they pretty much had Pennington at their feet. But they were never seen wearing their Presidential Medals. They didn't seem to be going for the attention most kids want; it was as if they were on another level. It was their parents who needed the attention; their mothers wore them around their necks to the market. Or carried them in their purses everywhere. And there are no real heroes today and they were heroes. What they did the morning of December 18 they did because it needed to be done and not because they wanted medals. That was the first thing that struck me as slightly unusual about all of this.

Why did I stay on in Pennington? What was the real reason? Was I suspicious? If so, why? Here we have a plot to wipe out most of the school by a bunch of morons called The Black Hands it was foiled by a brainy bunch of dilettantes called the Impromptus. End of story.

Every reporter bought it, except me. Why? I'm from New York for openers, and for another I'm a Brooklyn reporter, and to me the whole incident was too sweet. The Impromptus were in place waiting in the auditorium when the Black Hands appeared on stage and lowered their guns at the student body. If that scene had been in a movie would you have believe it? Not I. Sorry, I didn't buy it.

I called my editor and told her I wanted to stay on here in Pennington for another week. She wanted me back in the city. Story's over she said. I told her I wanted to sniff around. Nope. I told her I'd take my vacation time and if I came up with a good story I'd get it back plus expenses. "Something rotten in the state of Minnesota?" She said. "It's the cheese." I chuckled out of deference. I didn't have a thing to go on except vintage instinct. I knew something was brewing that was overlooked by all the reporters and I was excited. My wife was not excited. I could tell she wasn't. She called my motel at odd hours to check up on me.

When in doubt, I go to narcotics. I don't take them, I make a buy. I always learn something, and it worked for me here. I go to the right neighborhood bar when I want to learn, and most towns no matter how small have one neighborhood bar, usually a sports bar. At the off sides I made a buy. I called my shot carefully and came out pretty well. I told my dealer I'd need another ounce in a day or two and that by the way I was dealing cars, repossessed cars, and had a few steals. I told him my name was Joe Marco. Red was his. He knew I wasn't a cop because there were two cops in Pennington, a day cop and a night cop, and I wasn't one of them. I sat down with Red, bought him a few Moose Heads, and he asked me about the repos. I steered the conversation over to how much I admired The Impromptus, which wasn't a stretch. "Oh," he said, "they're not so clean." And he showed me some bad teeth and gave me a filthy wink. "I know one of them, a kid, he's all of 14."

"How do you know him?"

"He buys from me." And there it was; as they say in Hollywood, bingo!

"A kid of fourteen if you could believe it," he said. "Smart kid."

I played dumb. I didn't say and you sell drugs to him idiot.

"I admire the hell out of these kids," I said, "I'd really like to meet one. "

"Well this one dropped out of the Impromptus."

I said, "I'd like to meet him anyway."

"Be here tomorrow out back early and maybe you will."

Red was proud to be an enabler and the next night I was there standing in the weeds out back. Red introduced us. Marshall Sloan, one of the youngest of The Impromptus. Ex Impromptu. I joined them for a sniff. My party. I don't mind. I do it for the story.

I offered Marshall a ride home. When I got him in the front seat of my rented Chevrolet Neon, I snapped the child lock on the passenger door so I could have his undivided attention. I put the key in the ignition but didn't turn it.

"Now, Marshall. Can you keep a secret?"

Marshall nodded, looking ahead, bored. This kid was probably smarter than I was, I hate to say it but the rumor was that average IQ of The Impromptus was the boiling point of water.

"I'm going to say something that's going to sound scary, but if you think about it it's not scary at all."

"You're a cop." He said it as a joke.

"Yeah. Yeah, I'm a cop. I'm in from Minneapolis. Part of the guv's program to clean up burgs like these."

If he was surprised, he didn't show it.

"Prove it." Smart kid.

I whipped out my badge. I never leave home without one, it gets me in places we shouldn't be, and out of places we shouldn't be. He glanced at it. It was too dark to read.

"Is this a bust?"

"Not that smart."

"No, no, no Marshall, it's what you want it to be."

"So what are we doing?" He was bluffing but he was getting scared.

"We're just talking, Marshall, now, I know you're a bright kid."

I had figured out by now that he hadn't dropped out of the Impromptus; he'd been thrown for using. The Impromptus were clean. Martinis only.

"Joe, listen to me ..."

"I'm Officer Marco to you. Now as I said, I don't want to scare you, so just sit still." And just as I said it he grabbed the door handle, but it was locked from my side of the car.

"What do you want?" His voice was shaky.

I took a well-earned breath.

"Fill me in, Marshall. We both know you were thrown out of The Impromptus for using; maybe you want to share an anecdote about this little clique."

"Well, for one thing, it's not a clique." He handed me a business card. I read it.

THE IMPROMPTUS
A Gentleman's Club
Squire, Marshall Sloan

"So tell me more about this gentlemen's club, Squire."

"What's our deal?"

"There's no deal, Squire. Tell me what I want to know and I'll get a case of amnesia, capisce."

"And if I don't?"

"Your folks will get to read about your drug habit in *Time Magazine*."

"It's not a habit."

"Whatever."

"Well let me think about it."

There wasn't much to think about. I drove him home. We didn't talk on the way; all he said was that I should park a block down the street from his house. His neighborhood was made up of white columns, red bricks, and big old trees. I handed him the tiny plasticine envelope I'd purchased from Red as an act of good faith. He agreed to meet me at nine the next night, a school night, a block away from his house.

"I'll be waiting here in my Neon," I told him.

"If that's the name of your car," he said, "I'd change cars."

I liked his style. He couldn't get away fast enough.

Well, there he was there the next night. I watched him walking toward me passing under the street lamps, springy step. Nice kid. Average looking, likable. I guess he'd weighed the circumstances and seen that the scales were tipped in my favor.

"What's our deal?" he said when he closed the door. I started driving.

"Will you please stop bluffing, Marshall? I may have missed the Pulitzer prize this year, but I can tell when I got the dark chips stacked high in front of me. Now you got an axe to grind, grind it. Let me see some sparks."

"What do you want to know?"

"Nothing. Just start with the basics. It's a secret society, right?"

He nodded.

"Twelve members, right?"

Nod.

"You were the youngest?"

"By a month."

"So what did you do in that garage on Wednesdays?"

"Not much really. Talk, Martinis, chess, darts. Sometimes movies. Old music."

"Old music?"

"Like Cole Porter, Berlin, Gershwin."

"What movies?"

"We'd rent *Private Lives, Brief Encounter, Brideshead, A handful of Dust,* stuff like that. All from the 1930s. You know, Somerset Maugham, Fred Astaire, Malraux, Evelyn Waugh, Noel Coward."

I nodded at the jungle.

"We enjoyed a type of life that's disappeared. The point was to do smart things. Even be helpful."

I nodded. Go on.

He went on. "Like when Desmond found a bunch of books in the snow that some kid had tossed outside the library window he carried them around the building and stacked them in front of the library door. Stuff like that. They'd put out a fire. They always leave one of those cards at the scene. They try to right wrongs. They write letters. As a club they try to do good to carry a little weight."

I was just listening. "Tell me about your title, Squire."

"They all have titles, but that's secret, too. No one's really in charge, that's the good part. There's no king, but this guy Sebastian is a marquis. He's a senior. One of them is a baron and there's a count, you know, like that. We have an earl and a margrave. The new members are squires."

"Sounds harmless," I said. "Compared to other teenagers. A little weird, maybe."

"They prefer the word eccentric to weird," he said, "and teenagers are weird and into video games."

"Now tell me the hard part. Squire."

"Don't call me Squire."

"Okay Marshall, I want to know what was really happening on the morning of December 18 in that assembly hall."

"The Impromptus saved the school."

"That's right. And when they saw what was going down a couple of them ran and got the Uzis and the EC 9s and a couple of others got the Black Hands to lie face down on the stage. While a couple of others disarmed them and a couple of others filmed the whole thing from different camera angles. Am I boring you?"

"A bit."

"So?"

"So that's how it was."

"Right. And no shots were fired and no one was killed and the nine Black Hands, all of them seniors, are waiting trial for conspiracy to commit murder. And the twelve Impromptus from 14 to 17 sold their video tape, the whole event, to CBS for six-figures. And they're still running it on television."

"I got all that, Marshall, I filed that story, it's fiction. Now tell me something I don't know. Wake me up."

"Okay. I'll tell you what happened."

That easy. I'd poked a vein. It was as though he had been waiting to talk to someone. Something was on his conscience, whatever it was. Reporters and psychiatrists what can I tell you.

"They were outraged by Greenough's edict," he said. I hadn't known this but their principal, Mr. Greenough had forbidden the Impromptus from wearing their beloved linen suits anymore. Following all the other school massacres around the country Greenough made a proclamation that all gangs are prohibited from coming to school in any semblance of uniform. Simple as that. The Impromptus could no longer wear their traditional dress to school, off-white linen suits and Panama hats. Just as if they were a gang like the Black Hands, same category. The Impromptus were more than angry. They were the good guys.

He brought a tape recording of what he said was a faithful meeting of The Impromptus. It takes place November 11 in their rented garage at 735 Wilkins Street. This the Wednesday after the dress code proclamation, one month before they became national heroes.

He put the cassette into the tape deck.

"It's about 3 PM," he said. Wednesday."

He pressed the fast forward.

"How many present in the garage?"

"All twelve," he said without a pause.

He stopped the fast forward.

"This is my hearing," he said. "That's why I secretly recorded it."

He was asked to defend himself. He was honest. He had used cocaine. There was a secret vote. It was polite, gentlemanly, and a little sad. He was expelled for one year.

He skipped the tape forward. Stopped. Someone was talking about the Greenough edict.

"So how to respond to fiat rule that effectively robs us of our style? Shall we ignore it and just put it down to bad manners? Shall we write a letter to Greenough?"

I could hear the voices in the background.

One said, "I could kill Greenough for that."

Another said, "Spoken like a true Black Hand."

"Well, I could kill him, I'm serious."

"Yes?"

Someone must have put up his hand.

"It's true, it puts us in the same category as a dirty Hands. Who as we all know are sadistic morons."

"Count?"

"Who's that talking?" I said. The voice intrigued me, it was young and old.

"That's Sebastian. He was chairman that day."

"I too would like to kill Greenough."

"Alright, I think we all would."

"No. I was making a motion." I could hear a new young voice. I could hear laughter.

"Order. We have a motion made by Count Barton that The Impromptus kill Mr. Greenough."

"We must discuss it and put it to a vote."

I heard someone enter. Various greetings.

"Who's that?" I said.

"That's just Baron Desmond, he's our most affected member."

"Sorry, everyone."

"It's alright Baron."

"What'd I miss?"

"We're discussing a motion before us that we kill Greenough."

"Hooray. A sensible response to the edict."

"How should we kill him?"

"If you stop sniggering long enough I will. Greenough watches baseball every night at home. His wife goes to bed. Shoot him through the living room window. Okay."

"I thought baseball season was over."

"Baseball season is never over." It was Desmond's voice again.

I interrupted. "This is serious, right? Shoot your Principal watching baseball through his living room window?"

"Yes, of course." Marshall said.

"Have they ever done this kind of thing before?"

"No. And they took it to a vote, six to six, and I was asked to break the tie."

"You voted no?"

"Well, he's alive isn't he?"

I didn't say anything. I wasn't sure if he was kidding. These kids were neo-royalists.

"Tell me something Marshall. If the vote had gone the other way would you have killed Greenough?"

I waited a while.

"I honestly don't know," he said.

It chilled me because it seemed reasonable to him. He said it so casually I believed him. He went on.

"They'd have planted the gun in the right car and made the right anonymous phone call to the right people. It would obviously be the Black Hands with their moronic manifesto. They still throw bricks through windows and burn tires. The Black Hands are so obvious."

"What about jail?" I said.

"Oh Minnesota's okay on kids, they have a good juvenile policy."

He stopped the tape and removed it.

"What are you doing?"

"I'm taking my tape and going home. I've changed my mind."

"You know what I can do to you."

"I'm not as impressed as I was with you last night."

"Why's that?"

"You're not a cop, Joe."

"I'm not?"

"No. You're a real life reporter traceable through your bottom-of-the-line, cobalt blue Chevrolet Neon license plate FOM 834."

"That's my license plate?"

"You're registered at the Dreamland Motel, Highway Six under the name of Josh Marlowe. Your social security number is 532 24 0718. He said it from memory. You spent eight days in jail for perjury. May I call you Josh?"

"Yeah, go ahead." He'd made me with great ease. I was embarrassed.

"Turn it on again Marshall I can still write a follow up article"

After a moment he put it in. When it stopped there was a weird noise that sounded like a locomotive.

"What's that?"

"Martini shaker."

"Lovely sound." Suddenly I was thirsty. The tape chattered on in the background. "Did you do anything else at this meeting?"

"You'll see in a minute," he said. "We discussed, smoke, drank."

"You smoke?"

"Yeah. Lucky Strikes, Camels, like that, non-filtered."

"Why?"

"Well, they taste like cigarettes."

"So you meet every Wednesday in this garage. You sit around wearing linen suits and Panama hats smoking real cigarettes through cigarette holders, drinking chilled Martinis. You play chess, listen to Cole Porter, watch black and white movies, discuss affairs of state."

"If not us, who?"

"Is it true about the IQs?"

"It's not an accurate test, Josh."

"Just give me a number."

"The test is passe; they need to dismantle it. Nothing to do with instinctive intelligence."

"What's your number Marshall?"

It doesn't matter; Josh, with all due respect, I have a slightly better developed brain than most adults. I realize it doesn't make me a more experienced person."

I liked the way he told me that. It's not easy for a 14-year old to tell me he's smarter than I am without offending me. I could hear a Martini being shaken and poured.

"When are we coming to the good part?"

"Stay tuned."

"What inspired this club? Who was the brains behind it?"

"I don't think anyone. We all pretty much gravitated. We didn't trust anything; we trusted each other. I'll say this for it, I may have been the youngest but I wasn't ignored, the way kids are ignored in the real world. They listened to me. They're smart enough to know that age doesn't factor in with intelligence. We're all gifted and that's what made us outcasts. That's what the club was all about. Adolescents have always carved out secret worlds for themselves. And luckily there were others like me. Sebastian, Desmond. I have been very lucky to have friends I could talk with about something other than action movies and professional sports. They called us The Brainiacs. Well, Brainiacs are ostracized."

"What's your background?"

"Being a gifted child I was able to abuse my parents from an early age. Child abuse. Eventually they just let me be. They agreed to stop trying to manipulate me if I would stop trying to make them intuitive parents. By the time I was ten, I had looked around and didn't like the world I'd walked into, I didn't like the music, the clothes, the architecture, the art, the furniture, the politics, the cars. The style. There was no room for style. I had everything and as far as I could see into the future I wanted none of it."

"Were you nihilistic?"

"Well, I don't like that word, but in what sense?"

"That you rejected the ways of the world around you?"

"Pretty much everything that I was supposed to want I didn't want. I didn't believe what I was supposed to believe in."

"So what did you believe in?"

"I believed in before."

He stopped the tape.

"What about God?"

"God. Well God is man's greatest invention. After the lawn sprinkler and maybe the violin."

"Where does brain surgery fit in?"

"Brain surgery's good if you really want to live."

"That's nihilism."

"Don't call it nihilism Josh; we were desensitized. I wish I could understand what it's like. Not caring for anything, the normal future. The highly regarded professions, architecture, banking, lawyering, stock brokering. All of them phony. Do you know why a tiger eats its young in a zoo? She sees no possibility for her cubs. Call it nihilism if need to."

He said the word gravely as if he'd wondered. It was quite a speech coming from a kid who'd entirely missed Nixon. But it didn't prepare me for what came next. Nothing could have done that.

"So what happened next?"

"So last fall the school sort of came down on us. About a month into the school year it seemed that everyone had ganged up on us. The athletes called us brainiacs, the girls called us nerds, and the Black Hands beat us up. And then Greenough took away our right to wear our suits. Ridicule is a pretty powerful factor. Add bullying to that. We knew we had to do something. We just didn't know what it was going be."

"Did you resolve it?"

He nodded. He turned on the tape.

"At this meeting?"

"Listen."

I'm pretty good at uncovering plots but this one – well – this one frankly was beyond my experience for its utter brilliant perversity. As the tape turned the story came out. I couldn't believe what I was hearing. But as the voices chimed in one by one, each with a suggestion, they built a whim into a plan. It was military. It had soundness and precision.

Someone said, "We'll take it to a vote."

The vote was unanimous.

They were going to pretend to massacre the entire school. They called it Operation Scholacide.

"But why?" I asked.

"Don't you get it Josh?"

"To prove you could?"

"No, we were angry. Our rights had been taken away and we had done nothing wrong. We wanted to show them who we were, our potential power, that there was an elegant way to wield power. Pretend to massacre the entire school. Not just a few of them. Not running them down hallways and chasing them under tables."

"Whilst you were bored?"

"Of course."

He switched the tape on. I could hear some members laugh in the background. It was a joke. There were toasts. Martinis were raised. Martinis were swallowed. It was true. On the morning of December 18 The Impromptus would be armed and seated in the choir loft and stationed around the auditorium. At exactly 10:35 am the fire alarms would go off. The school play would stop. Sebastian's voice would come on the principal's loudspeaker. Everybody stand up. Do not panic. File out. Walk down the aisles to the exits on the right facing you. Do not turn around.

And four Impromptus would come downstairs and stand at the head of the aisles. All the exits would be barred except the one in front. The Impromptus would each be armed with automatic TEC-9s loaded with blanks. They would leave no room for heroics from the students or staff.

"TEC-9s? Chic," I said, "where'd you pick those up?" Marshall didn't bother to answer. It takes so little. Show up at any gun expo.

"So everyone would escapes through the remaining exit. There'd be no hurry; the stairs lead down to the Olympic swimming pool which is right under the auditorium. It had been contaminated the week before so it was empty."

"Contaminated?"

"Well someone put a large dose of hydrochloric acid into the filter system."

I didn't ask who.

"Everyone would be ordered into the dry pool. Students first." It reminded me of something. Being herded into a mass grave.

"Where did that idea come from."

"The Nazis. World War Two."

"Would they all fit into the pool?"

"Good question. An average person takes up one square foot. We'd figured ten percent would be lying down, some would have fainted and then the pool had ninety square feet to spare."

He stopped the tape.

"What about The Black Hands? Where did they come in?"

"Well then that was the big coincidence. Fifteen minutes before Desmond was going to set off the fire alarm to get the plan in motion low and behold the Black Hands took over the stage and trained their guns on the audience. Upstaging us. And they were serious. We found out later that their Uzi's were in place in the prop room locker backstage. Their plan was simple. In keeping with their brainpower. Messy and moronic. The firing was to come from the stage. Mow 'em down. There would be a lot of hiding behind chairs. Not a bright plan but then look at the source. Ours was a clinic in how to massacre a school."

"What was the Black Hands gripe?"

"All sorts. They were really pissed off about everything. We predicted they'd do something like Littleton but we didn't know when, of course. One of them actually said to someone, Kentucky, Mississippi, Colorado, California, Oregon, Arkansas, what about Minnesota? It's time we got on the map for something beside a governor who can beat the crap out of you."

"You mean they planned to knock off the school the same morning as The Impromptus. My that was a coincidence."

He nodded. "Actually the school assembly was the most obvious time, if you really wanted to think about it."

I still didn't believe him. Two simultaneous impulses to knock off a school. I mean how often does that happen?

"What are the odds?" I said dryly.

"One in twenty-eight point seven thousand. It was bound to happen eventually. Bad drama based on coincidence but you know, it wasn't that much of a stretch. America glorifies violent vengeance. Do I want a choo-choo train for Christmas or a Berreta. Which is the prettier toy?"

"Why don't I believe you?"

"Don't bother. The nice thing about reality is that it doesn't have to make sense. Fiction does. I guess the most wonderful part is afterwards when The Man in the Street takes his thumb out of his butt and says, how can this possibly happen? Oh I love that part. Well we all do."

I knew the rest. The Impromptus back stage saw what was about to happen and predicted the Hands next move. They were told to drop their guns which were loaded and still on safety, and lie on their stomachs until The Impromptus herded them down to the pool and pinned them with their TEC-9s until the police came. Everybody knows the rest but it's still pretty great stuff. It was quite a picture.

"Did you learn anything from this Marshall?"

"Yeah, I did. There was like a truly great enterprise. It... fascinated me from beginning to end."

"Maybe a little bit sick."

He paused for a while.

"Marshall?"

He squeezed his answer out. "Somewhat sick," he said.

"One more thing Marshall. When the entire school had been herded down into the pool what were The Impromptus going to do?"

"Go to lunch."

"Just leave them there. Lock them in?"

"No. Close the door. Head over to lunch. Village Chop Suey. We figure we'd be starving by then."

"How do you feel after telling me all that?"

"I have a sense of well being as a matter of fact."

I could have hugged him.

That night back at the motel I tried to make sense out of the story. Unraveling intricate plots is what I do. But here at Pennington it was huge. The two explosive plots intertwined. How good can it get? The Impromptus, from shining role models to degenerates. Distorted, corrupted but brilliant.

Anyway, that's it. That's my story that's all I've got. Just what I told you. I've already have 2,200 words. It's all on a disk. Click, click. Through the magic of telephonics my laptop is hooked up to my desk at the paper on 34th Street 24 hours a day and there it lies, waiting and waiting, for the early edition.

So I'm typing it now at the Dreamland Motel out on Highway Six I'm using my bed as a desk – I prefer it to a bureau. Give the Post a great story and I'll get my salary back plus expenses. I'm going to blow lid off Pennington. Prove all the reporters were wrong. And I like my headline. Bulky for page one in the Post, twenty-four spaces:

FROM ANGELS TO ASSASSINS. Ah maybe this would be better I still have to 5:00 am. HEROES TO SICKOS. Sixteen spaces, still too wide. Maybe this: GODS TO GEEKS. Eleven spaces, still a bit wordy.

I called my wife in New York and woke her.

"Hey wake up." I said it a little too loudly.

"Hah, ooh...where am I? Josh, what time is it?"

"Almost four, why?"

"Don't shout Josh."

I swore her to secrecy. I was whispering. I told her that The Impromptus were a bunch of sicko snob terrorists little perverts.

"I thought you liked them."

"I did. I do. It's a problem. They're out to prove a diabolic point." I told her the whole story, and that woke her.

"Look, I'm seeing Cyrelle in the morning," she said. "Do you mind if I discuss it with her?"

Cyrelle is my wife's therapist.

"Too late, it's in my computer at The Post ready for the early edition."

I could hear the television blaring in the room next to mine. Pow, crash, bang, explosions, death. Why can't I get a good bottle of scotch in this town over the weekend. Anything more than a year old. This stuff is from Filene's Basement. And I began wondering about this. About overthrowing the *Time Magazine* cover boys. About those kids weren't they heroes. And how much we need heroes.

And Marshall was right, the only heroes are sandwiches. And publishing my story would kill those heroes, ruin their hopes for going into any business life except computers. Disaster. And their parents. And what about the Man in the Street, whose hopes are dangling by thread on them. Doesn't he have a right to know, God love him. He's got a right to hear about his fellow man's illnesses as soon as possible, and that works wonders for him. Cheers him up, keeps him going. Take that away from the man in the street.

My problem is how do I feel about doing it. Fabulous, great.

This is a story sent to me by God. And next to God and the lawn sprinkler, the late breaking story is man's greatest invention and this is once in a lifetime for me.

This is Lord Carnarvon opening Tut-Ankh-Amun's tomb in 1927. But I don't know. Isn't it pretty much over. And didn't those kids really save the school; no matter what their motive was. And weren't they persecuted for being brilliant. There's a prejudice for today.

Pretty soon they'll be fanning out across America to class A colleges and so on and probably never come back to Pennington or ever see each other again. And if I blew this big shiny whistle none of them would ever get near a good college even on visitor's day. They'd be ruined. And they probably won't ever try it again, pretending to massacre a school, traumatizing all those people. Just a phase they were going through. Teenage phases; rebellion, dishonesty, sex, drugs, alcohol. The zilch generation.

The phases I went through were: shut up; eat what's in front of you; get a summer job; clean your room. But the Impromptus were role models for millions of high school kids. And what am I, a monster? Drop them into the cesspool with the Black Hands? I'm not the Red Cross but how could I crush the nation's illusions.

Yeah. Maybe I won't. Maybe I won't. I have a kill button

here. By hitting it I can delete the whole story. That little button is a pretty powerful little button. It drops the wings off the plane.

On the other hand I'm Josh Marlowe, a syndicated reporter and here in Pennington I discovered truth, where truth had no business being, and yeah the truth does not smell too good. And even though I'll probably miss the Nobel Prize again this year, I get another smell sitting here in my motel room on highway six just outside of Pennington a few minutes before sunrise on another clear April morning. I can smell a Pulitzer Prize and the smell reminds me of a rich – country – spring.

THE KITE STRING

The kite he found was in the shape of a bird. A sea bird or land bird, he didn't know which, but not a songbird, a predator. He'd seen it from a good distance, a couple of hundred yards, caught in a scrub oak tree and he had walked toward it, away from the path, walking through brush and new grass high as his knees, made high by a month of rain.

Now that he was closer to it he could see that the kite was out of his reach, barely snagged, high in the stumpy scrub oak, he felt a pang of good luck at finding such a treasure. He could see it was pretty new, no struts broken, the fabric was taut and there were no rips in it, though the colors had faded, maybe ble-ached by the sun. A fine looking kite.

He turned to scan the fields upwind to see if there was another boy walking toward him, expecting to see one, a boy like him, winding his kite string on a spool, ready to yell, Hey, get-cher hands off that. It's mine.

But there was no other boy, only the after-lunch sun, silence, and the wind hissing through the scrub and the grass.

Last year he'd found a kite blown for a mile, down a hillside caught high on a branch. He'd climbed for it but before he'd tossed it down to the ground he'd seen it was ragged, useless. Even the kite string was cotton twine and only a few yards were left of it.

This kite string was made of nylon, strong as fishline. He looked away from the kite, suddenly yanked it once from its source upwind, but it wouldn't come free. He tugged it harder and he felt the tension swell over a distance; it was snagged somewhere way out of sight.

A fallen kite string never falls straight. It blows with the falling kite, making loops, zig-zags, tangling on whatever it touches. But this kite string ran straight away from the kite, straight as a power line touching the tops of the bushes as far as he could follow it with his eye. He looked down along the kite string for a hundred yard until it disappeared.

He let the wind blow dry in his ears, deciding what to do, listening, watching, thinking. He was already late getting home. Should he cut it and take the kite without its string. Or should he follow the kite string to its source. Taut as a guitar string he felt its lure. He did not want to cut it; one does not cut a nylon kite string, or even tie knots in it. Anyway the length it seemed to be a perfect kite string of this quality would be worth something. It was a long one too, he could tell and he may as well take it all home with the kite, finding is not stealing after all. And a kite's no good without its kite string. It was nobody's kite and nobody's kite string. Finders keepers.

Still, he could not imagine why any normal kid could forget his kite in plain sight of the path. No one ever came here. Why would they? He hadn't. He'd always wanted to, he planned an excursion when he had the time to be adventurous, but he had never had gone this far down the valley. Maybe one day if his bicycle broke and he wouldn't able to ride the short cut home along the ridge road on top of the canyon. Now his front tire was flat and he left his bike at school. And here he was walking home. He didn't live close to the other boys from school who lived in regular neighborhoods. His house was off by itself down a dirt road in an undeveloped area at the base of the hills. His family did without television. All the other boys acted as if they'd been everywhere in the world and done everything because they'd seen it all on television. But none of them had done anything.

He stood a moment, then turned his back to the kite. He

pulled the kite again, hard as he could, feeling the tension spring back into it. It was as if it was fighting him. He pulled until the kite string slit the heel of his hand, thin as a paper cut. And he decided, glancing back, once at the kite. He took the kite string loosely in his fist and started to walk towards its source, letting it run through his hand with each step following its course, letting him lead it where it might.

The wind was down but the dry midday air was moving up to his face, warm from the valley, rising as it would all summer long from now on. He was used to playing alone, good at it. He never felt alone, or lonely. He played games with his invented characters. No one understands that you have to make up stories and people to keep you company.

Now feeling good and lucky, Special Agent Karl Strickland on his final CIA mission on assignment to trace the guerrilla kite string to its source.

The dark line of hills along either side of him seemed closer than they really were, but he could see tints of wild flowers among the scrub oak and sumac. Someone was watching him, of course, someone in the hills. He was being watched by his enemies, no problem, he was well armed. An AK 47 hung lazily under his arm from a shoulder strap.

He walked gradually down the canyon, its gentle grade, the hills to each of his shoulders, letting his hand run along the kite string, letting his hand pass through scrub oaks and green sage and bushes smelling of herbs he knew very well by sight but not by name, crashing through brittle greens making a way for himself, enjoying the tension he felt trembling in the kite string as though the kite were still flying overhead taking surveillance photographs of the missile site. And though the sun was high, he still felt the same cool rush in his stomach that he sometimes felt after dark when he hurried home for supper full of reasons for being so late. He was good at reasons. Once he told his parents that he'd fallen asleep in the grass and that he'd woken up when a pure white eagle standing on a limb near him told him that he was going to be late for supper.

"What did the eagle voice sound like dear?" His mother had asked.

"Like dad's voice."

His father had nodded but not smiled.

Now the boy was blinded by poison gas. He walked sightless head high only the kite string to guide him. No problem, he would get through holding his breath.

He stumbled and fell. Dots of blood appeared but he had not let go of the kite string. It was still. Only one sound, the warm wind rising close over the dry valley. An easy kite flying day. And still the kite string lead away from him leading him slightly downhill.

The boy had so few memories; he had stolen a little, lied a little, killed a little, a normal boy. It hadn't been more than two years since he interrupted his parents at dinner to announced that he had a penis. When he asked his father if he had one too his father had referred him to his mother who nodded yes. The men congratulated each other.

Daily life was still a surprise. What made voices come out of the radio? What was the wonder of ice cream? The utter kindness of dogs, the unfamiliar malice in movies. In the back of his mind he always preserved something to look forward to; no matter how far in the distance, there would always be a holiday.

Eyes open, his sight miraculously recovered through the use of infra red eye cream. He pushed along through the high grass and brush, more downhill than up, leaping a dry gully cut by many rainy springtimes, by the rush of rainwater running off the rooted hills down into the valley. He jumped another gully. The gullies were widening and deepening. He came to one he couldn't attempt and slid down into it, crawled up the sandy soil on the other side.

He scanned the hills for enemy binoculars. He looked back at his captured bird kite that was now no bigger than a ladybug. And still, at that distance, its colors flickered bright among the grey-green tones that came together at the head of the canyon beyond it, a mile back. He squinted ahead to see where the kite string might end. It dipped out of sight in the thickets. He felt the familiar isolation all spies feel on reconnaissance.

Not far ahead of him a hawk was making slow spires, calling out, riding the rising heat, making small adjustments to its wing tips, never once flapping its wings. A red-tail hawk, the sun glow dull, orange, through its feathers, red through its feathers. The hollow echo of its call. He answered, making the hawk's call. The hawk turned its head and looked at him. It swooped and landed on a bony branch in a rush of wings. The boy felt his spine tingle. The hawk called to the boy again. The boy answered, imitating the hollow call perfectly. The hawk and boy called back and forth and when he walked passed the hawk fifty feet away, he did not move. And when he looked back at it, the hawk was still on the dead branch watching him.

Wilderness: He's a hunter lost in the vast tundra of Alaska, his only friend is Crag, a young hawk who speaks to him only in riddles. His palm aches from where he had stumbled and fallen. Had he come too far; should he cut the kite string and turn around and go home? "No, where the kite string goes, so go I," he said it aloud.

He felt especially visible walking down the middle of the flat valley. Anyone with a decent telescopic sight could pick him off. I can cut the string anytime I want.

But he had walked too far. Even if he cut the kite string and turned round at that moment he would still be late getting home. I'll need something extra special today. Loyal to the kite string he played a game with only one rule: Never let go. He chanted again, where the kite string goes, so go I.

He was alone, and with every step he took he could not shake the feeling that a watcher was watching him. Nothing new. He was always under surveillance by his enemies. But today was different. This was an eerie feeling he had not felt before, and it did not feel like a game. It was hot. He was thirsty. An explorer, the last survivor of a Belgian expedition searching for the lost Roman wells at the Dakhla Oasis.

At the school picnic last year he pretended to be lost. He watched from a hill as teachers searched for him calling his name, again, and again. That night, the principal stood in his living room and reported to his parents the news of his untimely death at the jaws of a mountain lion who he'd surprised stalking the school picnic. "We all owe our lives to him," the principal told them. "You should be proud." His parents wept openly.

The boy walked another distance on sandier soil, the golden mustard plants high as his face, never once letting his fingers lose hold of the kite string, feeling it run through his hand, as he slid down into concealed ravines. The sun was blinding. The valley dropped off now, easing down, and the gullies widened into ravines' deeper than he was tall, and wider than his room at home. Nothing grew in the ravines' flat sandy floors and there were soft shaped rocks that had once been rolled there by rushing water of flash floods. And always holding the kite string at arm's length over his head.

Now he was standing on stage in the school auditorium, a gold medal on his chest held by a ribbon around his neck. The president's award for valor. A small bandage on his forehead. He'd entered the burning gymnasium and followed screams and somehow managed to force open an exit door, freeing the girl's physical education class, trapped by flames. Now the grateful gym teacher was speaking to the school, looking directly at his parents who were seated in the front row. "The bravest young man I've had the privilege..." (choke) she paused unable to continue. His mother was weeping. His father smiling, nodding, eyes shining. The gym teacher was only able to add - "An act of towering sacrifice knowing how much he hated girls. And the thankful girls smiled up at him through their tears. And the gym teacher's voice trailed off into history.

Now he saw the kite string disappear into a wide ravine and not reappear on the other side. Finally. It led down into the yellow glare of the sand and out of sight around a pear-shaped boulder, big as an elephant. He slid on his back down into the ravine and sat squatting on the flat hard floor in the dry heat, surprised at the deeper silence looking around him, slowing his breathing.

Another time when he had come home late he reported to his father that he'd seen a cobra headed swan in the Elkin's place and that if he hadn't chased it away it would have killed a dog. His father told him that he should carry a camera to record these sightings.

He could still see the line of hills overhead beyond the rim of the ravine.

He sat against the ravines wall, knees up, out of the wind. He was dry and thirsty. It was silent down there in the ravine. He had not once let go of the kite string. It led away from him, around the boulder into the black shadow between the boulder and the canyon wall. On a rock, close to his face, a tiny gray lizard winked at him.

He could barely hear it. A new sound he was not aware of at first, not the wind. A single high low melody, a single note. He listened, the sound was coming behind the rock up the ravine where the kite string had been leading him. It was the hum of a thousand tiny harmonies.

He pushed himself up to his feet and took several steps, holding the kite string, following the sound into the boulders' shadow, feeling the chill breath of stone shade. It was the hum of swarming flies. Now rounding the border but still in the shade, he saw close to his feet: a dead boy, who had not been dead very long; a boy, lying curled on his side, eyes shut, asleep, half in the sun, half in the shade of the boulder. His face was at peace. A swarm of flies massed where a small maroon hole flowered from his forehead. His blue-black hand was closed in a fist around the kite string. What will my father say when I tell him what I found.

The boy stood unable to turn away, even to look away, his head full of the awful roaring of the flies, the rushing wind in his ears. Then what he saw next, he saw in quick glimpses. In sudden mindless rushes. There was another boy just beyond the dead boy, not more than ten feet away a boy lying in a comfortable position. His arm and leg bones delicately balanced in their correct positions, as if he were about to rise to his feet and stand. The kite string wove through his fingers, through the phalange of tiny bones. And past him, against the sand wall of the ravine, and in its shade sat another boy, sitting, his head back. He had been there longer and the kite string passed through him too, mostly lost in the sand. Beyond him a clothed figure; the dire impression of a small human life held together by blackened ligaments a perfect hole in his skull. Always the kite string ran through his hand.

And further down the ravine, by a tenuous sage brush another seated boy, curled forward, had mummified. The kite string was tangled in the white tendons and grey-black bones of his fingers. His shirt was mostly gone, his head touched the ravines floor. The kite string led away from him still taut across a half buried femur bone. Around the rounded corner of the ravine out of sight. The boy stood rooted. Bloodless, stupid from the shock. Only seconds had passed. The blaring of the massed flies filled his head. He looked away. His mind flashing sense-lessly ready to run. The dead visions bursting through his mind and body like slow and continuous lightning.

My father will never believe me. He caught sight of movement at his feet, a shadow on the sand. The shadow of his own fist. And he raised it. he was holding the kite string along with all the other boys all the way down the kite string to its source.

And he began to open his fist.

Gardner McKay

THE GRIEF OF SHOES

My earliest memory is one of slanting sunlight on a grassy slope. Of small houses far away. Of being led by a woman's hand held high above me. We are following a path and there are clumps of trees. The sunlight seems faint. There are small houses on a slope.

I remember the scuffing sounds that our shoes make on the dirt path. As we walk, the woman hums my favorite tune. I cannot remember who the woman is.

I remember her shoes. She says they are new. Brown. In my secret language then, caca. They have laces and fat heels. I like to watch them beside my own shoes, which are white with a strap across the top of them.

I can see a man standing among the trees. In the shade. The woman stops humming. She yanks my hand. She turns, I fall over. She picks me up and holds me to her.

Suddenly I am squeezed between the man and the woman.

Then we are rolling on the ground. I am laughing. The woman is gasping. Then I'm all by myself, rolling down the hill.

They are lying still. I can't see the woman, because the man is hiding her, his hand is over her face. She is playing. She doesn't move. The man stays on top of her.

I watch her shoes. Her shoes are dangling in the air above both of them.

The woman looks at me. She is wet; her eyes and her cheeks and her mouth. I have never seen that before.

Then I take a nap. I wake up beside the woman in the grass by the dirt path under the trees. It is dark. She is asleep.

I remember being very hungry. I want to go home. I try to wake her. Her face is pink. I see drops of blood on her lips.

Then I am afraid. I put my hand over her nose and she jerks her head away. She is very angry at me.

We walk home in the dark. She doesn't hold my hand. I walk as fast as I can behind her to keep up. She says to me that if I ever tell anyone about the man in the trees, I will die in my sleep. But if I promise to keep it a secret, I will wake up and find a huge present at the foot of my bed. So I promise.

The next day when I am playing in the back yard, I see her putting her new shoes in the garbage. And then a ball of clothes.

Then in the morning, I see standing by my bed a red bicycle that I am much too little to ride.

THE FALLING WINEGLASS

She was certainly the most beautiful cellist in the world. He accompanied her, standing behind her, singing his long, clear poems that told us all where we stood.

They were a fabulous couple and very much in love. More in love than any couple I had ever known or might ever know.

They looked so much alike, both were lean-limbed, blond, always in motion, mustang-manes flying. They wore thin English raincoats on sunny days sometimes with nothing underneath. Deck shoes summer and winter.

They sat at the same cafe as we all did late afternoons for newspapers and ridicule, where we sipped all manner of European drinks, Pastises, Cinzanos, Fernet Brancas. I believe we all wore hats.

They seemed unrehearsed in our rehearsed world where passersby danced with an idea of themselves, people who constantly tried to snatch reflections of themselves from glass surfaces. So many glass surfaces in the city.

They did not ever stop being in love but were, always. Laughing loudly, sometimes bickering, only rarely throwing a glass across the cafe to emphasize a point. They were always, easily forgiven.

We rarely saw them apart. Apart they seemed vulnerable, wasted. She seemed distracted, incomplete. He seemed edgy, and incomplete. Together they burned like straw fire, yet we knew they'd never burn out. They were indestructible.

One summer evening at dark, as we sat outside the cafe under its umbrellas, letting the sweat of the day cool, we noticed bright gold rings on their fingers, simple bands. We asked.

We're married, they both answered lightly, not quite together.

We were stunned, so original. Nobody got married. We didn't think it was quite, well, decent.

We asked as if it were a tragedy: When did it happen?

They were laughing at us. Today.

Why hadn't we been invited?

It was so dull we thought you'd be bored. We were.

We forgave them.

They wore their wedding bands on random days; none of us could be sure if they were really married, or why. It was such a bizarre tour de force. Typical of them to set a fashion. We felt distanced for a time from this newly married couple, and we felt their power. Two of us married the next week, another couple the week after.

We all envied them. Their beauty increased with the weather, with each season. The summer was already hot, no one had air conditioning; and they were more beautiful.

Yet, what was it about them? They seemed to be more than just lovers, but what more was there?

That same month, July, one of us, a girl who was in love with him, crept through a window from the fire escape into their apartment. We never asked her what she was looking for. What she found in a bureau drawer under towels were their passports and between drawers, their birth certificates. She put them back and crept away. Late that afternoon at the cafe she had a revelation for us.

They were brother and sister. We acted unsurprised.

If anyone was shocked, none of us showed it. It was to be understood. We felt relieved by enlightenment and admired them all the more, what a feat. Twins. She was a moment older. It all made sense. That was their power.

None of us minded much, or so we told ourselves. Each one of us secretly desired one or the other, him or her, some both. I was fascinated by her, I never resented him. Did we act differently toward them? We never told them we knew; that was our power.

Now we saw the root of their permanence, the ethereal grandeur we couldn't have. We wondered what sex would be like between the same blood. Was the blood love of their love stronger than our love? Our love was between strangers.

We saw theirs as deeper fixed than ours; we envied them their permanent knowledge of each other. Their surface calm, their hidden emotions stronger for their concealment. What bond could be stronger than theirs? We might have been dancing with the idea ourselves; they were making love to it.

That August, when one of us was arrested for stealing a case of pineapples from the all-night wholesale market at 12th and Greenwich Street, they gave a concert for passersby to raise money for the bail. We barricaded West Ninth Street for a block and she sat on her stool in the middle of the street, her legs open to her cello and he stood behind her as always; they played high, to the open windows. Money fluttered down or was dropped into her cello case. The police came to remove our barricades, but just stood still, listening until their performance was over.

And that night, under the glowing umbrellas of the cafe where we sat late and drank the house wine from carafes, someone whispered in his ear, the wrong thing, and he threw his wineglass. He just stood up and tossed it high across the pavement. A beau geste, nothing more. I remember watching it rise then fall toward the street.

I never heard it break. I don't know what happened to it; it never reached the street. At the time, I wondered, but my curiosity passed with the night and I forgot about it. And the next morning in bed I remembered the falling wineglass. What became of it? I tried to hear it strike the pavement and smash, I tried to see the wine spread on the sidewalk, the glass shards scattered. But I couldn't.

Then someone started it. The whispering turned into a buzz. There was a blind item about them in the New York Post.

It would never get better and it was going to get worse. We didn't know which one of us had started it, but it was inevitable that someone would. Admiration to hatred is such a short ride.

At the end of that summer they left for Brazil where it was already spring. They sailed from Newark aboard the Holland-America Line. We all went to the boat party. As the ship slowly withdrew from the dock we stood below waving up at them leaning out over the rail of the boat deck holding balloons waving back, the wind blowing their raincoats open for us, showing us their beauty.

Each a beautiful creature. Can you envy love? Yes.

We never saw them again. Like wisps of smoke, stories rose out of Brazil, none of them true. They had gone to live in the north where the Tapajos River joins the Amazon, a small city with Portuguese and Russian and of course Indian people. An odd, old culture, yet one they could make their own and believe in, a perfect welcome. There was a coffee house with a billiard table near the riverbank and they say she often played her cello there for the people and he sang his words along behind her, in the Portuguese he had learned. They stayed for us always in their twenties. They died badly, that's all we knew.

I can still see the wineglass falling toward the pavement that it has never reached. I can still hear in the night the swooning notes of her cello descending from their apartment, all windows open, the breathless chords dropping down to the alley like vast silk sails, where in that dark there are so few lights, the senses focus together in harmony. I can hear his voice behind her, crooning, saying his words, speaking along to her music, while she emanates the rich singing sounds up up from the depths of their womb.

Gardner McKay

THE CROW WHO WROTE

❧

Once upon a time in a distant province named New Jersey in a township set among the plains and forests, there was found to be a crow who wrote.

And it happened that Carl son of Carl who had come also to be a cutter of meats as his father had been before him and his neighbor John who labored no more because of workman's compensation, came in their own good time upon a common crow whom Carl had caused to fall from its tree.

And it was soon enough that this common crow was to amaze all those who came to wonder, in the garage wherein he repaired. And soon it was the world that beckoned to this crow fully with promises of riches and good tidings.

But lo! In that season between winter and spring, neighbor came to be set against neighbor with tragic ends.

That might be a simpler way to tell you the fable of the crow who wrote, and if it hadn't happened to me, that's how I would tell it to you. But it really did happen to me and I'm the only one who knows, so if it is a fable it is a tragic fable. The local newspapers could only report it as an everyday crime. Television ignored it entirely. A fable must make some sense, news stories do not.

The Sesserwyles were my neighbors. Carl and Betty and from here on in I'll call Carl by his real name, which is Putter. I'm Bud.

In our nine years living side-by-side the Sesserwyles had done nothing un-neighborly. We kept a redwood three-quarter inch thick, seven foot high distance between us. We barbecued and during whitetail season Putter and I hunted.

With their children gone, his wife had returned to wait-ressing as much for spending money as to keep busy. He was a butcher and up at five each morning, drove a metallic hard-candy colored purple sports utility vehicle. He'd gotten a good price on it because of the color, but you didn't want to be close to it for long. I called it The Grape.

Putter's wife Betty bought all his clothes with the same hand that she had decorated their living room with, a room that made you restless very quickly.

Now that our children were gone, my wife Milly had decided to follow her dream of a career in opera which at forty-six was a bit of a long shot. The strands of our marriage had intertwined nicely once, but we had never quite decided how to tie them off and the arias were straining those strands.

When this crow business began, Milly and Betty were no longer speaking to each other; I don't remember why, but they loathed each other. Words been shouted across the three-quarter inch fence.

So what we had on the other side of the fence were the Sesserwyles, butcher and waitress, and on our side, diva and me-dical pensioner, me, with worker's compensation.

We lived in a good looking development named Somerset, in similar country estates with tiny lawns, identical gables, where no road ran straight, in a neighborhood that had appeared on sixty acres of potato fields suddenly one summer nine years ago.

And maybe because Somerset had been developed so quickly, my life there always seemed temporary.

I still believed that the future was mine, of course it wasn't. It was forbidden to me just as it was to every man in Somerset, the gate had swung shut the moment I signed the lease. And when I crushed my left hand on the job, I was laid off on permanent disability pay. I would never catch up. But no one I saw around me was really happy either. Maybe no one in New Jersey was happy.

Sometimes I would wonder about those men who went out in the evening for a pack of cigarettes and were never seen again. I understood that. So much for me.

The day it all started, the first Saturday in October, I was watching television, wearing a headset because of the arias coming from the kitchen; I think I was just switching between several sports, hockey, football, baseball, tennis, soccer, golf; their seasons were never really over. I saw the phone blink. It was Putter with a "let's go whitetail hunting tomorrow" call. I wasn't much of a hunter; Putter would go for whitetail; I'd go for rabbits. Usually we'd just take our guns out back and plink. That is, shooting at tin cans until they went plink. But that Sunday afternoon, a walk in the woods seemed like an excellent idea.

We drove north into farm country for an hour to a spot that he had found that had woods and fields for his whitetail and canals for my rabbits. He talked strategy along the way. In a vinyl case lined with sheep skin, he carried a very clean Marlin 30-06 with a one-fifty telescopic sight and could knock off a deer browsing in the next county. I never said it to him but I considered a telescopic sight the mark of a weak hunter and an invasion of the animal's privacy. But because Putter made the best rabbit stew in the world, there was no sense in making an issue of it and rocking that boat. I carried a Winchester .22 with a hooded sight.

It was cold. It was one of those dead sky winter days that seems to be over before it starts. The ground had been frozen and was undergoing thaw. Walking on wet ice on long brittle twigs partly stuck and unstuck dried leaves. Putter marched ahead toward the woods gun at ready. He wore a naval commander's beaked cap low over his eyes, and walked the proud leaf kicking walk toward the woods ahead to clear threat of deer.

He'd been a great athlete in high school.

I realized I was trudging, trying not to slip and fall. I wore a glove on my left hand, my bad hand, when I went hunting. Shooting wasn't a problem. I'd go to the canals where the rabbits hung out not far from the caves they'd dug in the embankment and could dive into in an instant.

We had agreed to split up and head off at angles and meet back at the Grape in three hours.

When I got back, it was three but the sky had already darkened. Putter was late. I had one plump rabbit in my game bag. I waited by The Grape. About 3:30 I heard a shot in the woods and after a couple of minutes, Putter emerged from the thickets, kicking along. From a distance it was easy to see he was pissed off. No whitetail deer adorned his neck. When he got closer I asked him what he'd just shot at.

"Crow." He said.

"You hit it?"

"I guess so."

That meant yes. I wondered why he'd want to shoot a crow. We ate what we shot and no one ate crow.

"What you shoot a crow for?"

Putter didn't answer me. It was because he hadn't shot a deer. Cold and angry he'd shot a crow as if he were plinking.

Without thinking, I started walking toward the woods and I entered them from the place he'd come out. In a few minutes I found the crow he'd shot. He hadn't killed it; there was life in it. A large crow the size of a chicken was lying at the base of its tree, a broken parasol, this odd bird, panting among the half frozen leaves, the noisy leaves, its dark eye glaring up at me. In shock.

Putter had come up behind me, he had tagged along.

"I guess I ought to do the right thing," he said.

"Which is?"

"Which is I wouldn't waste another shell on 'im."

With his boot-heel, he began kicking a rock loose from the frozen ground.

"You got him in the wing, is all, Putter." There was thin blood on the glistening black wing feathers.

"He's a dead bird. Bud, but I wouldn't waste another shell on 'im," he said again.

The crow had stopped struggling and lay still under us, my boots a few feet from its head. It lay on its side and blinked with its one eye which was dark.

"Maybe he could still fly," I said.

"Bud, for Christ sakes, it's a crow," he said as if to remind me.

"I know it's a crow," I said. "I just was wondering if it could every fly again."

"It's a dead crow, Bud, how's it gonna get off the ground?"

The crow snapped out of its shock and was on its feet with its good wing raised; its bad wing hanging independently. The crow flap-walked around in a circle. It glared up as us, black, stalking us back and forth, not trying to get away, but challenging us to fight, chattering adult sounds, rumbling. It was ready to defend itself on the ground, a pretty heroic challenge facing two huge men, one with a large rock in his hand. It picked up a twig and tossed it at us.

"I'm going to take it home." I said.

Putter looked at me. I won't forget the look.

The dark crow eye blinked.

Carefully, I picked him up. Wrapped my good hand around its beak. Trying not to hurt his wing. I pressed him against my chest, I got his blood on my jacket.

"He's fryer size, Bud."

"You want to cook him for dinner? You shot him, be my guest," I said to keep the conversation flowing. But it didn't. We walked back to the Grape in silence, me with the crow cradled in my arm like a baby and Putter glancing over at us from time to time, almost speaking but never quite.

"I wonder what it eats," I said.

"It's a crow," Putter said, "try garbage."

He had hunted badly. He had shot and not killed an animal and left it to die. As he saw it, I was trying to shame him. I wasn't of course, but there are rules. It was pretty bad between us, the worst it had been between us since we had become neighbors nine years ago and it was over a crow, but there was more to it than that. It was a question of hunting.

"You changed a lot, Bud."

I certainly had. Putter didn't understand this new twist in his old buddy, and his old buddy didn't understand it either. An odd feeling like a thrust of coolness had lifted through me when I saw that crow flick a twig at us. I admired it.

We drove the hour pretty much in silence trying to think of something to say. Our wives weren't speaking so maybe this was it. The end of a friendship. It takes so little, sometimes a brief phone call does it. Luckily the Celtics were still playing the Knicks so we listened to the end of the game on the car radio.

There's nothing wrong with hunting of course. Hunting well, that is. I don't have anything against it. Anyone who's ever lifted a hamburger and peered inside the bun and seen that brownish item, realizes that a living organism he knows little about, has died against its will. For him. Bon appetit. Hunting is just a more imaginative way to stop those living organisms.

Years of crankcase drips had left my garage smelling faintly of chocolate, more noticeable in the lush green heat of summers than the dry cold of hard winter. It was not an efficient workshop, just a place where my tools, tools handed down to me from my father, good tools, still good, were kept.

Above, the roof beams formed a false ceiling where bibelots of our past lives hung, not worth moving, throwing out, using, or examining, just things that were once indispensable and now were not. An iron floor lamp lay across a toboggan, planks from a long gone chicken coop, bundles of spare shingles. By my work table, a box stood on a long shelf window height. I stood, emptied rags out of it, and cut an opening in the side of the box and laid the crow inside. The garage was nearly freezing; I put an electric heater on the floor below the work table. The thin blood had dried on the crow's shining wing. The long black beak was firmly shut. The pale lidded eyes closed. The crow had not made a sound for hours and I'd begun to wonder if he'd make it through the night.

I asked Milly what she thought crows ate. "Corn," she said. By chance we were having it for dinner that night. She remembered crows stealing corn when she was a little girl. I brought him corn which I held in front of his beak and he refused. I set up a heater on the worktable and went to bed hoping to find him alive in the morning.

When I went it at 7:00 am he was sitting up in his box. I called Marty Dennis our dog's vet.

"How come you have a crow?"

"Never mind."

Marty seemed familiar with birds. He suggested I feed him a mixture of dog food, hard boiled egg, cooked oatmeal. I was to pry his beak open and push it down his throat with my thumb. Then I was supposed to give him water from an ear syringe. The crow's beak was a formidable weapon. A sword with a grip as hard as pliers, delicate as tweezers. But he accepted the food and water without a struggle, as if he knew.

That afternoon I drove him to Marty's. The first bit of news he gave me was that he was a she. On the spot, I called her Ruth; don't ask me why; I don't know anyone called Ruth. I don't even like the name. After Marty examined the wing he told me he might not need to X-Ray it and was pretty sure it'd be simple to get it fixed up with pins but to wait a week until she was completely out of shock. He gave me vitamin powder to mix in with her food and a delouser. He told me that crows were smartest of all the birds and that its intelligence would help it to heal.

I didn't see Putter that day or the next.

The next morning Ruth was sitting outside her box, chattering happily to herself.

I had a yellow pencil stuck behind my ear and when I leaned close to her she snatched it. It became her favorite pencil and she was never without it somewhere close by to her.

Sunday morning exactly a week since she'd been shot, Ruth seemed out of danger and was hopping around the garage floor dragging her left wing on the cement floor cackling flap walking, carrying a yellow pencil in her beak.

"Hi," I said when I came in.

"Hi," Ruth answered.

The vet said that this mimicking was not unusual but not to expect a very interesting conversation.

Now that she was hopping pretty well I made her a roost of rat wire mesh over newspapers that I could change daily.

The next morning Ruth and I said Hi to each other again. She made a sort of gasped abstraction out of it.

I noticed that she had pried open a wooden box of junk on my workbench probably with her beak, and had taken out a spark plug and a different pencil stub, also yellow.

I called Marty who told me that the pencil business was part of Ruth's foraging activity and that crows are notorious for stealing bright objects and that their favorite thing above all others is a yellow pencil. I gave her nails to play with and she did but she always came back to her yellow pencil. I bought a box of 24 and sharpened them. I doled them out to her as treats.

After I fed her I watched her snap up the yellow pencil and toss it in the air. She was chatting and playing. I sat and watched her play for half an hour. She always made me laugh. She was funny and brassy. Chatty, affectionate, constantly hungry but above all, smart.

Did she seem bored when she wasn't playing? I called Marty who told me to please stop calling him every time Ruth made a move but that yes she probably was bored because crows are overqualified for their place in evolution.

I didn't see Putter until the following weekend. These things are possible, close neighbors not encountering each other; it's just not likely. When I finally did see him he didn't ask about Ruth.

"The crow's doing great," I said.

He said, "Whatever."

"Want to look in on her? She cracks me up."

"Pass. I got to go the store." I guess assassins do not enjoy hearing news of the speedy recovery of their victims.

The wing operation was quick and simple and when Ruth came out of sedation with aluminum pins in her left wing she was cheerful and pounced on anything she saw, screws, nails, and, of course, a yellow pencil.

Ruth got to like it in the garage and usually had no fear of the people who came in. It amazed me, people were her deadliest enemies, hunters. But she could tell the difference. I brought my son and his wife when they came to visit over the Christmas holidays. She hopped over and poked them.

She would go still if there was someone she hadn't seen before come into the garage. But by the second time they came in, she greeted them. She'd poke her head out the window of her cardboard house and drop down and was soon fearlessly walking among their legs making deep curdling sounds. Dragging her bandaged wing at her side never seemed to bother her. She'd toss a yellow pencil at their feet. Or a nail. She'd even pick up a small screwdriver and carry that around, making deep unladylike cooing sounds.

She loved her yellow pencils but she never left any lying around. When I looked into her cardboard house, there they were, neatly stacked at one end.

Finally, it was our dog Remy's turn. Remy was a big calm dog. He was made up of Labrador, German shepherd, French poodle. I had intentionally kept the two of them apart, but I'd become more and more anxious to see how they'd react to each other. Remy was very confident of his place in our world. He would either welcome Ruth as a guest to our household or he might eat her. One morning I brought Remy in and tied him off.

When Ruth saw him she froze. She opened her beak and raised it to him taking a defensive position. Remy was fascinated. Maybe he sensed that he had frightened her; anyway, he turned away and lay down with his muzzle on his paws and closed his eyes. He had never done that, I'd never seen him do anything even close to it. She hopped over to him in her friendliest manner making her deep coo-ooing noises. Unbelievably, Remy kept his long muzzle on his paws and with his eyes barely open, blinked.

The two became friends and it wasn't long before Remy let Ruth climb on his back and with her there, stood up. Ruth hopped forward along his back and stood on Remy's head gripping his ears with her feet. They stayed like that balanced, Remy with a mild smile on his face. I couldn't move. They walked around the garage like a small circus act. I wanted a witness, but I was afraid that if I called out for Milly that she'd jump off.

It was a Sunday afternoon six weeks after I'd first seen Ruth half alive under that tree, it was now Christmas week and the weather at night dropped to well below freezing. But the sun was hot coming through the garage windows though the temperature outside read 30 degrees. I'd moved the heater up onto the work table near her box. Now she could spring from the work table to a chair to the floor. Now she could get back up. I was just standing by the workbench I don't remember why or what I was thinking; maybe I was just enjoying Ruth's activities off somewhere clucking.

That was the day I first noticed the pencil marks on the wall just above the work table. A scrawl like a two-year-old might make. I was pretty sure they hadn't been there before and I knew that I hadn't made them. They were simple up and down strokes, a continuous MMM. Just a few inches above the work table. I didn't call Marty. I remembered what he said about crows being overqualified. She's so restless she gets bored. She would try any- thing to relieve her boredom.

I looked in her house. There were the pencils stacked neatly at one end, ready for use, one was on the floor.

It was time to patch things up with Putter. I had to show him what was going on in the garage. I went next door and knocked. Betty came to the door and pointed. A game was on in the living room, I forget what it was.

"Putter," I said.

He kept watching the screen. He didn't seem surprised.

"What'll it be, Bud?" Faintly hostile.

"Nothing much," I said.

"I got an eight point whitetail the other day."

"I know."

He'd gone hunting without me and come home with buck. He'd sold most of the venison so he wasn't offering and I wasn't asking.

"Want to go crow hunting, Bud?"

"That's cold." I said. He still resented what I'd done.

He turned and looked up at me.

"You didn't answer me."

"Hey, Putter, let's get over it."

"I am over it, Bud, are you?"

"Let's call its quits, Putter, I'll buy you a beer."

He came over. We sat in the kitchen and turned on the game. He didn't mention Ruth, I didn't either. Milly was singing La Boheme upstairs in the bedroom with the door open. I closed the door but it didn't help much, the aria leaked through the floor. So we went into the garage and I showed him my new chop saw.

Ruth was in her box. She poked her head out, curious. I wondered if she'd remember him and she did. She ducked back in and froze. Putter wasn't exactly her best friend. I did not attempt any circus acts.

I took Putter to the work table. Together we stood looking down at the marks on the wall. The MMMM went on quite a ways.

"That's a lot of Ws." he said.

"It's Ms," I said, "And I didn't make them."

"I hope not."

"Ruth did."

"Ruth?" he said.

"The crow."

"You call her Ruth?"

"Yeah, and she hops up here, picks up a pencil and writes on the wall."

"I believe she's trying to communicate with us," I said.

"Is that possible?" he said.

We thought about that for a moment. The evidence glared at us from the wall. The delicate line made by millennia of misunderstanding between the species.

I didn't see any tears of remorse, but I saw what seemed to be respect at the patient's progress. He seemed interested but was trying not to show it.

We hadn't seen her yet, but all the time she'd been watching Putter, waiting to get him, waiting for him to do just what he was about to do, bend down over the work table, within range of her. Suddenly she growled like a dog. She was out of her box beak open, pecking at Putter's eyes.

He ducked his head and covered it with his hands. She was completely out of her box, flailing her wings, and without opening his eyes, Putter took a swipe at her, a lucky one for him, an unlucky one for Ruth who went skittering in a morbid half skid, half flight along the garage floor.

Without thinking I hit him, I coldcocked Putter from behind with a rabbit punch, catching him behind the ear and sending his head back down to the bench but it didn't stay there; up it came spinning around toward me and he clocked me one on the ear that rang my bells and down I went but I didn't stay down; I kicked his legs out and jumped him. I wasn't even thinking. He was punching up, I was punching down. Then he was on top of me. Next thing I knew Milly was screaming at us in that expensive trained voice of hers.

"Stop, stop, don't do this; oh that horrible bird that horrible horrible bird," like it was from La Boheme or something.

Putter stopped punching and shoved me. He'd had enough

but he wasn't beaten.

"You're gonna regret this, Bud, you son of a bitch." And he stormed out of the garage and as far as I could see, for the rest of my life. I was still lying on my back with a bloody lip and a busted head. I heard Ruth chattering. She'd been huddled in the corner the whole time, ready to die again. I got to my feet. Gently I picked her up. The wing looked okay. Quietly I talked to her, "It's okay, it's okay" I told her in a soothing voice, "It's okay, Ruth." I touched her behind the head between her wings where she liked me to and she pretty soon she gave me a warble and a bit of chattering. And I brought her out some fresh chicken livers.

Putter had once given me a roll of butcher's paper so that night I tacked a length of it above the work table by Ruth's continuous MMMMM. I took a black felt pen and made a large A on it. She was watching me and chattered the whole time.

The next two mornings when I went into the garage with her food. There was no mark beside the A. But the following morning, there it was; she had made an A. It was shaky but it was definitely an A. I brought her another chicken liver and she clucked deep in her throat. Of course I couldn't have known it then but it was this letter A that was the beginning of this whole horrible tragedy of the crow who wrote.

That day, I drew a large B on the butchers' paper and tacked it on the wall beside Ruth's A. I didn't have long to wait. In the morning there it was, a shaky letter B. And soon she had given me C, D, E and eventually the alphabet from A to Z. I stood her on the bench and wrote her name out several times on the wall. R-U-T-H.

A month went by. Then one morning, I saw little delicate lines beside her name. She was trying to copy her name. I got a chill on my arms. The marks were clearly staring back at me from what depth I couldn't guess.

I hung a seven-watt night-light over the work table so she could see what she was doing at night.

A savant such as Ruth could never do more than this, could she? Was this the start of a conversation between bird and man she was trying to begin?

She had gotten so used to Remy she would wait for him, and as her wing healed she would drop down on his back. The look on his face was one of pure contentment. He'd lie down and let her groom him with her beak. Dog and bird, they were a happy pair.

When she wrote the name REMY I was surprised but not overly.

It was time to call Marty Dennis. I brought her in. He checked her wing and decided that all she needed was exercise and she was ready to fly away. I asked him how long she would live. He told me that if I kept her she could live another 15 or 20 years but free she might not do as well. When I unrolled the sheet of butcher's paper he thought I was kidding him. He didn't believe me. Then he was overwhelmed.

He said it was a very significant step in interspecies communication. He had heard of cases where crows talk, count numbers or pull up fishermen's lines and strip them of fish, but this, he said, went beyond that. The next day he called Brooks Institute. They referred him to the ornithology department at Cornell University. Cornell requested photographs of Ruth and copies of the marks she had made. They were easy to photograph. I shot a roll of film by the window. I didn't want to frighten her with a flash.

The Cornell professor answered me immediately. Would I drive Ruth over to them so they could examine her? He said that she was a phenomenon and as such needed to be studied over time.

I said, No. I told him I'd have to drive through Pennsylvania, not a good route, a couple of hundred miles through back roads. And because his department wasn't going to reimburse me or put me up at a hotel. I told him that if he wanted to see her he'd have to come down to Somerset, New Jersey, where Ruth lived.

He said he would.

Meanwhile, I had contacted several talk shows. The letters went like this:

Dear So and So,

As we greatly admire your television show, acting on the advice of certain parties, I am writing to share with you the phenomenon our crow, Ruth. She is exceptionally smart.

She can write words. She can write the word THANKS HELLO BUD PENCIL and so on. I suppose she stands on one foot and holds the pencil with the other foot. She loves yellow pencils and steals them whenever she can. We have told almost no one about this. If you would like her to appear on your television program please contact me at the above address.

The David Ryan Mister Midnight show was the first to answer. A Fed-Ex Overnight Letter.

Mr. Ryan is extremely interested in your writing crow. As you know, he has built a small part of his reputation on the indiscretions of household pets.
We would require an audition of your crow in our offices and should we agree to slot him on our program, we would be willing to pay you 2,000 dollars plus travel expenses, meals, and first class hotel accommodations for you and your spouse. Please ring Dick Brevvy, our Talent Coordinator. I will bring him up to speed on your crow that writes. Welcome to Show Business!
    Sincerely,
      Don Tony

That was better. 2,000 dollars. It was a dream. Accommodations at some hotel like the Essex House off Central Park. Great food. Fame.

Somerset doesn't have its own newspaper, but somehow there was a leak. The Cold spring Current ran a piece based on what I told the reporter when she called. The paper was making a fuss over Ruth. Channel Three drove their truck over from Patterson to our driveway and put Ruth on the evening news. They called her a scientific breakthrough.

People I hadn't seen since I'd been on the job came over and watched Ruth snatch shiny objects, spoons, spark-plugs.

In all this time Putter still avoided me. Gone at 5:00 am setting up his meat counters, home after dark. I never saw Betty. They were through with me.

Ruth seemed very content. Well enough to be set free but without the desire to do so. I had decided to let her go after the David Ryan Show. I'd seen her collecting rags and sticks and nails and all manner of things and getting them up to the rafter above her worktable. She would spend more time up there than she spent in her cardboard condominium.

But throughout her building activity, she did not ever stop writing. Each morning I would find new words, sometimes a short sentence. Marty looked in on her. Now that she was a celebrity he was making house calls.

He told me that the nest building activity in the rafters meant that she was pregnant. She would delivering a clutch of eggs sometime that month. The David Ryan Show was off for at least a month.

Ruth chattered happily to herself, pregnant and thriving, she would stare out the garage window and talk at wrens and blue jays who would look startled and fly off.

Finally I found four perfect bluish green eggs splotched with brown in her nest. It made the Patterson Herald.

Ruth's news value had soared. Everyone knew where she lived and there was the question of security. I know New Jersey well enough to know that someone out there would be willing to kidnap her. We didn't have an alarm system and Remy was a sound sleeper. For the month I decided to sleep in the living room with my .22 rifle leaning against the door to the garage.

It was ten minutes to five, the first night I slept in the living room, when something woke me. Out the window, I saw the shadow of a man slipping between Putter's house and mine, then opening the back door to the garage. I took my rifle and snapped the safety catch forward. Without a sound, I pushed the kitchen door open with my bare toe. The garage was dark. I saw the man's outline at the work bench. I was shaking.

"Freeze," I believe I said.

The intruder turned. There was something in his hand. I couldn't make out what it was. I fired once. I heard a gasp, then a horrible groan. He fell forward hard over the workbench. I heard his head strike the cement floor. I waited. When it was absolutely quiet again, I turned the light on and went over to where he lay and turned the body over. It was Putter. Dead. I'd shot him right through the heart.

I sort of collapsed and fell backwards and sat on the floor for a long time. My head was spinning so fast it felt that it had come off. I was in shock. I was panting. I just listened. The house was quiet so was the neighborhood. Milly must have slept though the shot. Finally I got up. Ruth was safe on her perch.

The gun in Putter's hand was a chicken neck. In his other hand was a yellow pencil. A bag of chicken giblets lay on the floor. A key to the garage lay on the floor not far from him. I'd given it to him years before so that he could feed Remy when we went on a cruise.

He'd been doing this all along, sneaking in on his way to work, writing words on the wall to make me look like an idiot. Ruth wasn't a savant, she was an average crow who liked yellow pencils.

I took the pencil out of his hand and tossed the giblets up to Ruth's perch. She hadn't uttered a sound until then. I went into the kitchen and called the police. I didn't even wake Milly.

A horrible mistake has been made. I shot him. I was breaking down by then. Saying it aloud had made it come true. A neighbor returning a tool. Or borrowing one. Anyway a neighbor in my garage. I shot him. Mistaken him for a burglar.

There was an investigation, but by that evening it was closed.

Putter's odd little joke of vengeance had gone far too far and had taken his life. I never told the police what I knew, or even his wife who put their house on the market and moved to Florida.

The eggs hatched soon after. When the baby birds first opened their eyes I helped Ruth move them into the nest in the tree behind the house. She even let me help with the feeding. In a couple of months they were flying. They never flew away. Nor did she.

It's early summer now. I'm watching Ruth out the window. She's in her nest, two of her fledglings pestering her. If I walk out back she'll spread her wings and drop down on my shoulder and get chatty. She's very smart.

But she's never written another word.

TOM

৵◌

Sometimes during the dry, rustling summer, a lizard would drown in the dog's water bowl left out on the brick walkway. Whenever that happened, Michael would discover it first thing in the morning; a finger-sized lizard, it might have drifted to the bottom of the bowl, pale belly upward, frail, its tiny arms spread, its excellent hands palm-open, fingers wide, reaching. Always peacefully asleep, and always disturbingly beautiful to Michael.

At breakfast he would report the news of each drowning to his parents, who were kind enough not to take the news lightly. The world, after all, had been diminished by one lizard. They shook their heads gravely, smiled at each other when he looked away. After breakfast Michael would bury it in the burial plot that he'd cleared at the foot of an arbor post, reserved for drowned lizards.

On certain nights, after he had gone to bed but before sleep, Michael imagined how these lizards drowned. Thirsty, a lizard would strut out across the bricks in the moonshine sensing water nearby; it would make a sudden lizard-leap to the rim of the dog's water bowl, gripping it with its thready fingers. Michael imagined it leaning down to the water's still surface until it kissed its own water-shadow. Then, its neck puffed out, it would drink. When it was full, it would fling itself away down to the brick walkway and skitter off.

Michael always tried to keep the level of the water close to the top so that a lizard could drink safely without leaning too far down and falling in the water. But sometimes on windless mid-summer nights, long after Michael was asleep, Mick, the dog, would lap the water low. And maybe later a thirsty lizard leaning out and down too far, would suddenly find itself alone in the middle of the bowl, splashing to keep its head above water. its fingers too smooth against the bowl's stainless-steel sides. And so another lizard would drown.

Michael was haunted by each death. Following each burial he carried with him the torment of the lizard's final struggle, he saw it thrashing in his day-dreams again and again, against the stainless steel cliffs. Reaching for the rim above the slippery sides was what haunted Michael most; though he never told his parents, he somehow felt the fault for these deaths was his.

One sultry mid-summer morning, Michael discovered a tiny boy in the water bowl. A perfect boy, no bigger than a lizard. A boy dressed for school and very much like him, a miniature reflection of himself. The boy's arms were peacefully open, fingers spread, his eyes were closed, his face was calm, asleep.

Immediately Michael wanted to reach into the bowl to touch him, to pick him up between his two fingers, the same way he would pick up a drowned lizard. But he was afraid; as he reached down he stopped. He could not touch the sleeping boy. Instead, he ran to get his father, who was shaving, and by the time he'd convinced him to come to the bowl, the tiny boy had turned into a tiny lizard.

The next morning, it happened again. When Michael discovered him, he forced both his parents to come and look. Too late.

Days passed. Michael longed to see the little boy again. Then, following a long hot night a week later, there he was. Michael sat down on the brick walkway beside the bowl and stared at the boy. How could any boy be that small? He felt relieved, sitting close to him, as though he belonged there beside the sleeping boy. Why did the boy look exactly like him?

He knew that if he went away from the bowl, the boy would turn into a lizard. He glanced away once at a bluejay curious about whatever was going on in the bowl; it was time enough. When Michael looked back into the bowl, the boy was gone and a lizard was there in his place.

Michael's father was uneasy over the imaginary boy, and, as his mother told him at dinner, in an instant of brilliance allotted once in awhile to fathers, he dug up a round, flat-bottomed rock, washed it, placed it in the center of the bowl so that it formed a dry island any lizard could swim to, clamber up on, crouch, drink, then leap away to safety.

Michael never found another drowned lizard and he never saw the sleeping boy who looked just like him again.

But some time after the dry rustling summer had led the countryside into a mean frost, Michael's mother would wake whether there was a moon or not, sit bundled in the window seat near the bed. And if his father woke, she might say something to him about Tom, Michael's twin brother, reach out for his hand with an old longing, now wondering whether or not Michael should be told about Tom, and what happened to him years before, when the twins were babies, left alone by their nurse in the steadily rising water of the bathtub.

GRACE AND QUALITY

He had always loved her and she had always ignored him, pointedly. Feelings of the heart must be made precise in a small town where hope is nourished by closeness. Especially in the small Louisiana town of De Grasse, where there was no getting away from each other. Feelings must be decided from childhood.

And in every other aspect that counted to Lucy McGrath, she simply felt superior in every way to Elwell Thomas: smarter, finer, richer, nicer-looking. So for the benefit of Elwell and the town's witnesses, she remained firmly aloof from him. Still, for years, he kept a clean, blue-flamed torch burning for her. He'd had one of those childhood crushes that had not been extinguished by time. It had aged but hadn't matured.

Lucy had been aware of Elwell, of course. She had eyes. How could you miss him? He'd been the all-state athlete in three sports in high school, and now she could see him most any day hanging around at odd times, saying Hi, Lucy, or gaping at her from across the street from the First Louisiana Bank Building or outside McGrath's Mall, studying her, wearing one of his many checked shirts, as if the checked shirt was an important fashion statement.

Lucy was town royalty because she was heiress to the only shopping mall in De Grasse. She had gone away to Ethel Walker School up in Connecticut, then south to L.S.U. in Baton Rouge, and had come home with a degree in business to manage the McGrath Malls. She'd had a quick sophomore marriage no one in the town knew about, divorced, graduated, and now she managed the three shopping malls, one in town and the other two in Sharon and Monroe City. She drove between these three locations usually at well above the speed-limit. And drove desperately, it seemed to Elwell, driving her small Lancia convertible that could only be serviced in Baton Rouge.

Elwell had stayed put in De Grasse after high school; he'd gotten a job because he couldn't think of any better way to support his parents. He wasn't good looking cinematically, but he did have an ample head with generous features, a fine man's head that didn't depend upon ornamental hairdos; a head that would look complete later on when his hair thinned. At Podvol High School, mainly because of his head, he'd played the King in Hamlet. Lucy, home from Connecticut for vacation, had attended the play and met him backstage afterwards. He might look like a king, she had said later, but he sure didn't think like a king. She was quick to notice quality: Not one of us.

But neither was Lucy McGrath noted for her great beauty; she was a mite too thin, the witnesses said, she wasn't keeping herself to advantage. She wore her nice black hair pinned too flat. Still, Elwell thought she was the most feminine woman in De Grasse. She always wore dresses and he'd never seen her in town wearing jeans. What she had was quality.

Elwell's main personality trait was that he'd always been far too easygoing; he was even at peace with himself, which no one who knew anything was, thereabouts. And he was not ambitious in any known conventional manner; to Lucy McGrath he was everything small-town she detested. Especially because he's an adult male who still rides a bicycle, for the love of God.

The 12:01, pulling out of De Grasse late, was accelerating from its stop back in town, overdue five minutes because of a delay in cooling down the generator. The engine was gaining speed, being driven back up to its full drive in long even strokes. The powerful rolling motion of the engine rocked along its length as the great weight accelerated away from town, down the tracks toward a small, bright automobile, slick as a wet bar of soap, stopped off a dirt road with its left front wheel locked between the main track and the switch track.

It was the mid-point of a perfect, long summer day, a heavy-lidded August stillness hung over the woods, bugs stood in the air above the warm grass, an easy breeze blew across the tops of the fields. Tall stands of pines posed, deeply shadowed by the noon-high sun. The gossiping birds abruptly paused to listen when they heard a strange new sound.

The shrieks of the engineer's warning whistle welded Lucy McGrath, where she sat behind the steering wheel. Her hands gripped it, all ten fingers riveted. She stared at the oncoming train as though it were an unannounced caller coming up the walkway to the McGrath mansion at dinnertime. She was in a spellbound state somewhere between her cloudless life and her immediate death. And her immediate death seemed inevitable.

Elwell's people, the Thomas family (pronounced gar-raunce), were descended from Cajun stock and had come upriver to De Grasse when his father, Pitou, was a baby. Elwell'd grown up in a poor, isolated class and had kept to himself. An advanced case of richly deserved humility, Lucy McGrath had once said. He keeps a red canoe tied to the top of a Ford car that doesn't even work, parked under a huge cypress tree and his idea of a big fantasy is to get off by himself and try to make that thing drive him to some impossible-to-get-to lake for the weekend. She once said to a girlfriend that she was still waiting for Elwell to unleash his awesome mildness upon the unsuspecting world.

He would never again apply for a job at McGrath's Shopping Malls, Inc.; once had been enough. Their serving maid had reported to Elwell that Lucy's father had brought out Elwell's job application at breakfast, saying that Elwell reminded him of the mechanic on television who tells you your muffler's shot. When Lucy had laughed, he reminded her that Elwell was also a first-class athlete. Lucy had snapped that Elwell might be a first-class athlete but he was second-class everything else. Her father had said, "That's all we can hope for in the shipping department, hey, Sweet-pea."

"Papa, I heard he fell off his bike once and hit his head on a rock and ever since he's had the brain capacity of a chicken."

Her father had laughed, "Sugar, there are some pretty smart chickens out there, now ... "

"Not in Elwell's case, Papa, There's nothing going on inside that chicken head, is the trouble." And he had dropped it.

It was fun to be Lucy McGrath as long as you could go to Antibes in the spring and ski in Colorado Springs after Christmas. And speed around in your neat, Lancia convertible from one deferential branch office to another. After all, Lucy McGrath was a crowned head, De Grasse's only true Princess.

The train was fascinating to watch in the distance, seen from the fields two miles away. A farmer, Ray Soulette, who also liked to watch trains pass, stopped working as he did every day at this time. He liked the way a train seen at that distance moved so slowly. He checked his watch: 12:11. Late. The train was shimmering in the heat rising from the glinting tracks, its miniature four-eight-four engine hauling a line of tiny cars up to speed from the town station. He called to his dog and turned away. He'd be going up to the house for lunch now.

The warning shrieks from the engine, L-O-N-G short- short L-O-N-G short-short, did not enter Lucy's brain. Her reflexes had gone dead from panic as sure as if she'd had a stroke.

Her people had founded De Grasse in 1802. Tigue McGrath had been a slave owner since Napoleonic times, before the Purchase, and he founded a Scots merchant family of quality. The only time Elwell had seen the interior of the McGrath's colonnaded mansion was at their Decade Party, given for the townsfolk. There, in the library, Elwell had gazed around him at the

grave leather volumes that had stood for scores of years unopened, to be perused at some invented day in the non- existent
future. He tried to imagine living with Lucy in the house as man
and wife. Unable to do that, he had decided to get drunk on the
magenta doch-an-dorrach, made of sparkling wine and tropical
punch, served from a crystal basin in the great ballroom with its
stained mirrors. Later, successfully drunk, standing in line to say
thank you and goodnight, he leaned against the foyer wall, facing
the McGrath family. When his turn came at the front portal,
Lucy gave him a small, hard handshake. Gripping her knotted
hand, Elwell had drawn her toward him, off- balance, and
grabbed her cleanly by the back and waist, and with years of
longing behind him, had kissed her wetly and surely on the
mouth. She'd had no choice, of course, and when she had freed
an arm, slapped him smartly across the face.

Two years before he graduated from Podvol High School,
college representatives had begun to trickle into to De Grasse to
watch him play. They offered him scholarships, asked him to
enroll here and there. When he passed them up, Lucy McGrath
had written him off as a complete fool. Small towns need fools.
They need heroes as well. But Elwell was never comfortable as a
hero, setting himself above his friends. Off the field he'd been
shy, as if his clear advantage over other athletes embarrassed him.
He might never amount to much, but to anyone who'd ever seen
him play a sport, he would always be remembered as an athlete
of supreme grace.

He loved natural things and was comfortable with animals;
uncomplicated, wise to some but not many. His great sports
years had ended in high school and he'd only ever played for the
thrill that his speed and reflexes gave him, same as a dog who
leaps high for a flying disk.

The farmer Ray Soulette heard the whistle blast L-O-N-G
short-short L-O-N-G short-short L-O-N-G and turned back to

look. He'd never heard the train whistle before. He scanned the tracks ahead and saw the small white car with its top down stopped on the tracks by a dirt road. He figured the distance closing between train and car at less than a mile. Up in his field where he stood the train's screams sounded cranky and full of resentment, sounds that a powerful beast might make when it is no longer able to control its destiny. When he saw a person sitting still in the car, he felt powerless, useless. Get out, he said quietly, Jump, jump, jump. Please.

Lucy'd had visitors to De Grasse. Over the years, self-confident young men had come to stay at the McGrath estate for weekends, usually during the summer. Serious men in suits who looked casual in the distance. Elwell would watch her and her visitor, squinting half-hidden from a field or road, as she walked along with a man he'd never seen before, maybe hand-in-hand, and he'd ache, wondering if this man would be the final one. But then he would never see him again. And in all that time, Lucy had not spotted Elwell observing her. He decided that her pretty eyes were to be seen, and not to see from.

Now, Ray Soulette heard the lightning screech of steel-on-steel as the engine's brakes slipped on the smooth track sending fire-storms of sparks flying away to either side of the tiny engine. And the useless braking burnt the wheels and could never ease the train to a stop at that short distance. Now, pushed along at full speed by the loaded cars it was hauling, they drove its engine forward with their tons of inertia. On it rolled, swaying, the heavy clackety-clackety cars driving on behind the engine. Nothing could stop the engine and its cars until it had rolled a long way beyond the stuck car.

Once or twice a week, Elwell would ride his bike down to the tracks outside of town where the valley widened into fields, just to watch the midday train pass. In its massed power, he felt a relentless destination, New Orleans, far away, enigmatic as the great ocean beyond. He felt drawn away from De Grasse as it swept by. Or especially late at night if he was awake and heard the Limited up from New Orleans speed through the sleeping town without slowing.

The screaming engine was now less hundred yards away.

Elwell threw his bicycle down, leaped the sheeny rails to Lucy's car, reached into the front seat across her legs, unclipped her seat-belt, and with his arm around her waist freed her from her car, easily ripping her out of it over the closed door, out and away from the tracks and down the embankment. The three seconds it took Elwell to do this was divided into dozens of moving parts.

It was a calm feat of precise grace, witnessed only by a terrified engineer leaning out of his engine cab, and a farmer on his way to lunch, stopped in his sweet potato field two miles away, who even at that distance, marveled at its clarity and speed.

Even before Elwell and Lucy rolled down the slope, he heard the ripping sound of the wrenched fenders and doors flung away to both sides of the engine, then a quick explosion, the car's gas tank. Her pretty little foreign car was debris.

Down they tumbled, locked together, down the dirt-grass banked grade and lay there entwined, stopped in a green gully, hidden by leafy shade, on mattressed grass.

The car had been flung away on both sides of the track into the cottonwoods, and the screaming engine had been slowed and finally stopped far down the tracks.

Faintly, Elwell heard voices in the distance of crewmen and passengers stumbling back down the tracks toward the dismembered car, with all the bright excitement that attends disaster.

Lucy lay, eyes closed, trembling from shock. She seemed slightly aware, but peaceful. Elwell's slowed seconds quickened back to normal time, and he felt his breath join hers. Carefully, only moving his eyes, he looked around.

Most of her dress had been torn free, maybe snagged on the triangular wing window, and what was left of it was high around his own waist, and one of her legs lazily gripped him. He had dreamt many times of being this close to her.

He lay there nose-to-nose with his sleeping Lucy in a mild euphoric state, feeling her shiver, not wanting to move, afraid to alter the delightful aftermath, aching, not from his tumble, but from the euphoria of his sudden entrance into the privacy of Lucy McGrath.

Waiting for a gift had usually exaggerated hope for Elwell, but in this case, waiting so many years to be this close to Lucy McGrath had contorted hope into stunned paralysis.

In the moments that followed after they'd come to rest, the overhead birds, no longer startled, resumed chittering, informing each other, beautifully describing their fears and warnings again and again. And the sound of flying insects grew back to its symphonic hum. Elwell was trying to breathe calmly, feeling an ecstasy he'd never felt winning any game, and something clicked in the back of his mind; it came to him that all his victories had been useless by themselves, that this was what his heroics had all been for. He'd only been in training to save Lucy McGrath's life.

They lay half-hidden in leopard shade, neat as lovers, as though they'd been this close for years. Elwell's right arm was stuck under her, gripping her waist. She was askew, wrapped around him. In her loosened hair, he scented sweet shampoo, and below her neck, traces of the chic perfume she'd crossed herself with after her morning shower. With his brusque chin, he touched the pale, perfect skin of her cheek, breathing her bouquet, letting her breath enter him. He felt her cool moisture. She was still shivering. He drew her to him, just barely, with his right arm. His free hand still lay across the back of her knee.

And with the roaring of large, strange bells in his ears, he felt his free hand drift naturally up behind her thigh, slowly up, lightly skimming the edge of her panties as it passed, suddenly close on her buttocks. Then he firmly pressed her entire body to him, feeling the warm life in her.

"I love you, Lucy McGrath," he said aloud, without knowing it.

Her pretty eyes opened slowly, one inch from his. She drew back slightly and recognized Elwell at once. She smiled at him, realizing she was alive, and felt the sudden warm whoosh of euphoria.

"Hold me, Elwell Thomas," she whispered huskily, "I am alive and you saved my life."

She pressed herself closer to him than he thought possible, braiding herself tightly around and between him like a bitter-sweet vine. Her smile turned into a silvery laugh tinged with emotion and he laughed with her. He fell back on his elbows and laughed. She crawled over onto him, grabbed him and kissed him well. She was no longer laughing and yanked her silk blouse away from her body and wrapped her legs around him again. But he couldn't stop laughing all the while they were kissing each other and rocking back and forth, rolling around, flattening the long grass, making the love he'd imagined them making for years as he had drifted off to sleep so many times alone in his upstairs room.

Lucy opened her eyes slowly.

She focused on Elwell's eyes, inches from hers, she recognized him instantly; his nose, lips. He was smiling dimly. The grass beneath her felt cool, still damp in the morning shade. The close fury of the train had left her breathless, thankful for life. What am I doing here with him, of all people? Then she remembered: He saved my life.

She became aware of fingers, not her own, gripping her nether regions. Then movement. Pressure against her vagina and breasts. The brusk stubble of his cheek, his breath, the weight of his shoulder. Pleasurable.

Lucy felt high. Suddenly she threw her leg over Elwell's hips and mounted him, quickly as if he were a galloping roan stallion, clinging and grinding, needing him to penetrate her for all the years he hadn't. But just as he was about to enter her, she felt herself release and give; she came abruptly, frantically, then fell away.

Now, she felt his weight above her and opened herself beneath him, spread and gripping, and she submitted her years of restraint to his cock. As she watched the great simple man above her, shoving himself in and out of her with all the strength of the four-eight-four engine that had nearly killed her, she now realized that she'd always wanted to feel it his cock, she'd always wondered. And now she knew. She gave herself fully and took everything he gave her, slipping back deeply into her dream, she felt herself coming and coming and coming ... falling and falling.

A few minutes later when the engineer spotted them down the embankment in the clearing under the cottonwoods, his first puzzled thought was that they were in agony, writhing in some sort of death spasm. They were locked in such a churning embrace, legs and arms and extremities clenched, convulsing. He had never seen anything like it.

It was an image that was destined to haunt him during the idle moments of every day for the rest of his life.

Now, Elwell stirred. He had stayed within his dream for only a matter of seconds. When he came to, he lay facing Lucy, less than a yard away. Her dress was up around her chin. He felt blood in his mouth and dripping into his right eye from a cut above it, followed by a pang of sickness from his concussion.

As he had leaped free of the tracks like a rustic Superman with Lucy tucked under his arm, he'd fallen blindly over the embankment, using his own body to cushion her fall. When they glanced off ground and were still falling fast, he'd cracked his forehead on something, he didn't know what, maybe a tree stump. He slipped unconscious, but they'd kept tumbling until they had rolled to a stop under a stand of cottonwoods. He lay a few feet from Lucy, who'd fainted from fear.

As he reached out and touched Lucy's clear calm forehead, crumbs of black dirt tumbled from his fingers onto her eyelids. They flickered. He instinctively moved his hand down her body to pull her dress back over her legs, but allowed his hand sag and rest on her upper thigh.

"I love you, dear Lucy McGrath," he said quietly to the sleeping girl.

Lucy was swimming in dreams just below the ice of consciousness. She heard a voice close to her. In her dream, she remembered Death crowding her face. She remembered sitting in her car, wheels stuck, the growing size of the dark engine coming toward her in all its splendid details, a shimmering figure of Death. She saw the sparks, heard the shrieks down the tracks. The trapped, awed feeling closing in on her face. Unable to move. And she heard her own voice say: It's simply too pretty a day to die.

She'd been distantly aware of her car's brief explosion, and had begun dimly to realize that it had probably been obliterated beyond any repair. Still afraid to open her eyes, she was coming back to her place, in this world, in this time, in this town.

Now she remembered she was Lucy McGrath and she wondered what she would find of herself. She felt her arms, rubbed her legs together, and realized she was intact. With her eyes still shut, she slowly ran her fingers over her face. She saw a vague glow flickering through her eyelids. She became aware of fingers, not her own, gripping her buttocks.

She opened her eyes slowly. Lucy focused on Elwell's eyes,

inches from hers, his nose, lips, she recognized him instantly. He was smiling dimly.

"Jesus God," she whispered, "You!"

And in a burst of righteous strength she jerked herself free of his arm, shoved his face away from hers and did her damnedest to scratch him, her hand fanning dirt from the tip of his nose. "How ... how dare you?"

Trying to get at least one foot under her, she staggered backwards and fell, prettily he thought, clean white-pantied, knees high, into the matted grass. She lay there unable to cover herself, fearfully glaring at him between her raised knees, fully exposed. Excited, flushed, panting, and more beautiful than he'd ever imagined her.

"What in the name of God was it you were startin' to do to me, Elwell?" She glared at him as if he were a gelder of pigs, "Rape me?"

He studied her a moment. He shook his head and smiled.

"Filthy hands all over me," She panted. "Takin' advantage of me; Elwell, you are indeed a mess; you are poor, downriver Creole trash."

"Not Creole," he grinned, "Cajun."

"It's no better, and what difference could it possibly make?," she panted, breathlessly correcting her mistake, "Excuse me; you're God-damn Cajun trash, violatin' my, my, my human rights."

This was the longest sentence Lucy had ever spoken to Elwell, and in her voice he heard her generations and satisfaction and well-being.

Lucy had still not covered her body.

"My, my. You about finished, Lucy McGrath?" Elwell was enjoying her long-legged and disheveled snit.

"Pure trash," she repeated, looking away.

"Pure Cajun trash," he corrected her. He grinned.

"Don't you go gettin' any fu'ther ideas, Elwell Thomas," she said, "And quit grinnin' at me like that. You're grinnin' at your betters."

A voice hollered down from above the trees.

"You alright down there?" The engineer himself, with two other men, barely seen through the thicket of cottonwood.

"At last," Lucy sighed to the sky above Elwell. She struggled to her knees, covering herself, holding her blouse together, her skirt with other.

"Help me, please, somebody." Lucy yelled back, "I believe I'm just fine. Now why don't one of you kind gentlemen come down here and help me back up the hill?"

And she turned and slapped Elwell hard across the face. As hard as she had at the McGrath's Decade Party, as hard as she could, anyway, from a kneeling position.

THE SEA WALL

႞ၜ

A dream is waiting for us resting on its wings
beneath the sense we prattle and try to make of things.
A dream as sweet as morning is bitter as a weed
and every dream is fiction, the fiction that we need.

It was bad where he had been and it was bad where he was going. The road ahead was lost in the rain, the windshield wipers were sun baked and hardly interfered with the rain, they combed the rain and made blurred moments when there was nothing ahead and he imagined a dog, wet, heading home, confused by his headlights trying to cross between his sizzling tires.

The rain was coming off an ocean gale that had blown itself loose across the island. He felt as if he were pushing a small boat through a storm at sea. The entire island seemed to be sailing through it.

Something small was on the wet pavement ahead. He stopped. A frog. Hop pause hop pause. Its pathetic openness, giving him the rights to its fate.

It was a bad night. He had not wanted to drive, but he had had no choice. He had had to get out. He was jarred by where he had been; they had clashed, and he could no longer stay there. It was late.

There were two ways out of the city. Driving home he had chosen the slower way; a couple of miles longer, it was a route that got away from the main highway and wove through dark residential streets.

He had no destination, nowhere he wanted to go. But he had not wanted to drive. He drove too slowly.

The road ahead of his windshield was fluid, in a pause between wipers he saw it. There it was. Too quick, rippling in his headlights, almost at his hood, he slammed the brakes. Too late. He was sure he had hit it, something small. A pale shape. His windshield wipers had left him to guess.

Stopped, in the gusts of rain. He left the motor running and pulled the handbrake on. He felt a sickening surge. He sat in the car as if he had anchored his boat in the storm.

He had heard nothing; there had been no thump; maybe he hadn't hit it. Whatever it was there was hope that he had imagined it, that it was not lying in the street ahead of his car. But yes, something had been there; hadn't he seen something through the blur? A small pale shape? God, what had it been? He sat in the stopped car.

After a long time, maybe a minute, and hoping it was not a dog, he opened the door and let the wind yank it forward from his grip. With his hand on his head holding his hair dry, he walked around to the front of the car.

He wiped the water from his eyes. There it was. In the drizzled refractions of light just under his front bumper he saw it. It was not a dog. It was a child. It lay on its side half under his front bumper, sheltered from the rain, it lay like a stunned bird. He stared down at what he had done, engulfed with rising sickness. Was it dead? Of course it was; he had struck it with a car. Rainwater blew down the back of his neck and ran down his spine.

It was not a baby; it was a small child. Lying on its side. Its hair was light colored, curly and hung down longish and wet in the back. where the rain had splashed. It was wearing tiny overalls, Lying as if it fallen asleep in the shelter of the car's grille. No bruise, no cut, unmarked. Was it a boy or a girl?

Sick and desperate he backed away to one side of the street over the curb, bent down and vomited on someone's lawn. The house beyond the lawn was dark; they were all dark, not even the flicker of a television set. When he stood up again his mind blurred. Why couldn't he just lay the body along the side of the road? People did it all the time with cats. For a moment he considered it; it would be easier. What time was it? Past twelve, no, past one. What difference did it make?

He walked back to the car; with one hand for support he went around to the hood and stared down at the child again. The overalls were pale colored; were they blue? There was a whale or a hippo sewn on the bib between the straps. There were yellow ducks and piglets on its T-shirt. He decided it was a girl. He wasn't a good judge of ages; it could have been as young as three, maybe four. So small.

He went to his knees and gently, gently pulled her forward and raised her, fresh, still warm, limp as any sleeping child, but not calm asleep, calm dead. He put his right arm under her spine and with his left hand he opened the back door and laid her along the seat. He wanted to touch her chin.

He would never remember what thoughts were storming though his mind in those moments; they weren't even thoughts; they were impressions of terror. He had killed a child.

All he ever remembered about those boiling moments was turning the handle of the back door and admiring the ducks and piglets on her T-shirt and that it was a hippo on the front of her overalls. Why couldn't he go to the office in the morning wearing hippos ducks and piglets sewn on his own suit? He tried to settle his raging brain.

He spotted a beach towel on the floor behind the seat and draped it the length of her body; it covered her easily. He wanted her behind him while he tried to think; he did not want to see her face, an attempt to put her out of his mind. And not a good one.

There had been no dark pool of blood. No wound that he

could see. He guessed that he had been only one inch too late, that his car had stopped when it struck her, that the bumper had barely smacked her and she had simply toppled the way a bird does when it has flies into a window.

His car was stopped between streets lamps. He switched the motor off, then the headlights, and sat in the front seat of the dark car parked on a dark street in a neighborhood that had gone to bed. No car had driven by; no light had come on in the houses on either side. He knew he would be ashamed for the rest of his life, that every morning through his remaining years he would feel the anguish he felt now. He sat in the dark car. What to do? He took his pulse, his heart was running at a smooth 180. Was it Thursday? Of course it was. What time was it? Past one? He looked at his watch, ten minutes after two. 2:10 am. No it was Friday, early. He did not exist. It had not happened. He looked around to the back seat. It had happened.

Tears like sweat wrung from the corners of his eyes. There was no grief in his tears only a savage anger, hatred for himself and his eerie ability to destroy. Then he began to cry fully, sobbing first out of self pity, then mourning for the baby, for her parents. He faced a great empty ocean of remorse.

If he had wanted to go home, to his house, he would have simply driven home, the normal way. But he hadn't done that, he had wanted to postpone his arrival. In spite of the weather he had chosen the wrong way to drive home and driven to this spot from an address he was never destined to return to. As if by app-ointment, he had arrived at the place where his life would end again, tonight its turning point. Tomorrow his life would no longer reproduce itself.

The road not taken, he said to the dark car.

It gets down to that. If I'd taken the right road, this would never have happened. If, if, if. If Grandmother Rose had six wheels, she'd be a bus.

Over and over, churning the words, I was driving slow. Tumbling through his mind, It wasn't my fault!

What to do? That responsibility. Inside the howling car he tried to think. Go down the street house to house knocking on doors? Call the paramedics? He was relieved he did not have a car phone; he was able to postpone whatever responsible act he should do. He would need to drive to a telephone. He'd passed a bright telephone hutch a mile back in front of the Royal Food market. Call them. Why not?

Because the paramedics would contact the police. They would question him. Politely at first because of the car.

"Where were you driving? "One of them would say.

"Home."

"Where were you coming from?"

"None of your business of course, but Ann Stribbling's house."

"The name rings a bell."

"It does doesn't it?"

"Wasn't she married to Marshall Stribbling?"

"Yes she was. And so what."

"Did you and Mrs. Stribbling consume any alcoholic beverages?"

"Did we drink, detective?"

"Can you say, Did you have a couple of drinks with Mrs. Stribbling?"

"No? Okay then, between the Beluga caviar, the pate de foie gras, the smoked wild salmon, we managed to swallow half a dozen Martinis and two very chilly very large bottles of Veuve Cliquot."

One of them would tell him to breathe into a small pipe with a gauge attached. He would read the gauge and drop politeness.

"You're legally drunk, sir."

"I can see why you made detective."

Handcuffed, he would be driven down to the police station in the back seat of their patrol car. The trip would end in a room lit more brightly than any room he'd been in recently. A Policeman would take his picture, another would hold each one of his fingers paternally while he rolled them in ink and printed them on paper. Another would give him a tissue to wipe the ink off them. He would be told to remove the belt from his trousers, the laces from his shoes. "Why would she have even been there, detective? A child crossing the road in the rain at 2:00 am?"

"I'll write a letter to the judge."

And so what had been one instant of dreadful blindness would become a malicious felony that would last him forever. He would become the poster boy for the public, the rich drunk in the German car, the perfect example of what can happen when you drink and drive.

"Lock him up. I hope you like your suite, baby killer, you'll be in it a long time."

No, it wouldn't do to call the paramedics.

He glanced at the back seat. There was the beach towel, the small mound. Just as he had left it.

He was terrified. For himself of course but as he sat there in the dark car the blind drumming rain he became terrified for the mother and father terrified for the funeral terrified for the spoken words of a child that might have been. For a man may die but a child may not. A child's death remains an appalling mystery. The untroubled beauty of a new soul facing out. A small person who has not yet learned the ways and tricks of behavior, who has not yet grown accustomed to the low price of hatred, absorbed the atrocities common to daily life, who cannot possibly guess the conditions of how she will be treated, or learned to believe that there is no alternative. Still, death is not ever due the just arrived. Dying is far more becoming to the scarred than to the unscarred.

The waves of rain sweeping by made a pleasing sound thrashing the roof of his car. He slipped under; passing out, he ran and hid in sleep.

A voice woke him.

"It's crazy what you were trying to do tonight."

The voice of a young girl. A young smart voice but whose was it? It was coming from inside the car.

"What?"

His head snapped around. He could barely see in the gloom. There was no one there.

"What was I trying to do tonight?"

"Replace her. You can't, she's dead," it said.

If he had been drunk he was now sober. He faced forward and turned on the dashboard light, he rubbed his face punishing it as if he were drying it with a burlap rag. When he was done he looked into the rearview mirror as if he'd seen an illusion, a trick.

His eyes had gotten used to the dimness. He hardly heard what she was saying only that she was saying it. He answered the voice looking into the rearview mirror.

"I'm getting on with my life."

"It's no longer your life. You had a life and now it's over. So you can't get on with your life."

"I'm doing fine."

"No, you're not. You want to get on with a fake life. It isn't fair to her."

He felt his mind drain, his vision darken to grey, just before it went black he was able to hear the voice say:

"You two were the difference between diamonds and pearls. She's gone."

"Yes," he tried to say.

His head slipped of its own weight, his shoulders slumped, he dropped sideways onto the seat beside him.

In his dream he drove the car away much too fast. Trying to get free. So fast it seemed to fly. There was no sound. The child was beside him. Her unguided soul flying through his night to an unlisted country.

His dream. He felt it to be the safest madness of all; truer than himself, the dreamer, truer than what he would find at his feet when he woke. The dream was the only time he knew, and he would never know the dream when he woke from it. A new life, a destination. In it there was no more rain no more steep hills no more grief. No more inventions like Ann Stribbling to murder his nights. And it would always be there like the sea waiting to grab him.

"Wake up, daddy."

He did. With a start.

"I want to go home."

He turned. The child was standing on the seat behind him; her head poked up out of the beach towel. In the dim circle of light he caught the glint of her eyes, light clear eyes, her small uncomplicated face, her lips. Thank God. He couldn't speak.

"I want to go to bed."

"You're okay."

"Sure."

"But didn't I hit you?"

"No you did-n't."

He watched her speak. She was staring directly at him, mink

eyed, her mouth open, waiting for him to answer her. Was she smiling?

"You're okay?"

"Sure. Are you?"

"Yeah, I guess."

"Why did we stop here?"

"I don't remember. Maybe I was too tired to drive."

"What are you crying about?"

"Everything."

"Don't cry, Daddy."

"Okay."

"You miss her don't you?"

"I do."

By the time he'd driven up the hill and parked in the garage she had fallen asleep again. He lifted her still wrapped in the beach towel, breathing nicely, and carried her to the front door and unlocked it.

He had left lights on inside the house but there was no woman. The house reeked of absence.

There was only the baby, her cheek flattened against his arm, her lips pressed to one side, she slept at peace, as if sleep were the sweetest place she could ever visit.

When he laid her on the bed and pulled the blanket over her, she stirred and made a tiny chirring sound.

He sat and dropped his shoes on the floor and lay down beside her.

He was large, she was not.

And for the time, he became a sea wall built to stand between the baby and the impossible black that waited for her beyond the room.

PROVENANCE

From under the house, the red chicken blinked once at the man then charged. It flew beak first, directly at his face, scanning his cheek with its wing, throwing him off balance, down, backwards into the dust, the hard dirt floor of the yard. He'd forgotten about the Waimanalo chicken; tough moa, the mothers of professional fighters. Kai'ea looked around to see if the taxi driver had witnessed his huli. The taxi driver had driven off. Kai'ea was alone.

Sun, sky, noon. Everyone gone. The small unpainted house. The yard still green, shaded, wild, choked, half-dead, half-alive, parched. Leftover rubble from old people too tired to move it or throw it out.

There it is. High overhead, coconuts ready to drop, ka'u keiki niu, his baby tree. The day he was born, his father planted it. He told him, "Kai'ea. You can never be as tall as that niu, but try to have the good sense a tree like this will never have."

When he was two or three he'd asked his father, real cute. "Will I grow coconuts like my niu?" Makua kane had scooped him up in his arms and told the story a thousand times.

As his tree grew tall, Kai'ea grew tall, both of them straight, but he did not have the good sense his father had wished for him.

Now. This tree is all I have left of the old man.

Hello, niu, you lookin' good.

It does. It rises forty feet on a sweet arc out to fronds ten feet long, from the dust below he can count three dozen fruit.

Remember my name, niu? Kai'ea Porter. I come home. I served my time, now I can make something out of me, nothing can stop me now.

The key's hidden where the nurse told him it would be, under the ole shell. The house is an abandoned museum, piles of folded letters, small hand tools, fragments everywhere, dried *ti*-leafs hanging, plates on chairs. The house smells of many scents, all of them old.

Here is where my father died, in this bed. The sheets are clean, un-ironed, the pillow flat as a penitentiary pillow. He touches the bed, I brought shame on you, fadah. He turns, looks around startled by the sound of his voice. I come back home.

Home. Single wall construction, three rooms, rolled tar roof, short stilts, and now it is his. Ka'u keiki hale, his childhood house. Mama tried hard to sell it for makua kane's medical costs but no one wanted it enough, and anyway, he'd slipped away pretty quick once he'd seen the tests. If I had been here, if I had been here ...

Hidden under the house, lies his board; he can see its shape in the gloom outlined against the nodding lattice. The fine rocker, the broken skeg sharp as a breadknife.

He'd carved it himself when he was thirteen, fiber-glassed it, surfed it during the fidgety years before he ran away from home. It's lain here hidden, untouched. Twenty-four years.

He'd been edgy growing up at home, I'd seen a better life somewhere else, yeah? On the permanent hype of television. He was no longer straight like his niu – always a problem. He'd smoked grass in elementary school, LSD in junior high, batu in high school. Then he was gone.

His memories collide now without concussion.

On the mainland he teamed up with a biker he'd met at the beach, a mechanic from Tacoma-Washington a couple of years older than him. He'd gone with his sister. They dealt batu, with samples and demonstrations of the product.

The three of us started in Tacoma, then Seattle, we crossed to Boise, dropped down to Salt Lake City, on to Dallas, then the compulsory Los Angeles, capital of scam; In a week I could make my cut a thousand dollars.

I got a strong whiff of mainland prejudice; no one ever knew where to place me but they went ahead anyway, between Native American and Hispanic.

But I'd gotten a life: a car, an arrest record, a woman; I was not yet eighteen.

The police called what we did recreational crime, dealing, shoplifting, it led naturally into armed robbery. The three of us, we called ourselves Bonnie-and-Clyde-and-Clyde.

One day, shots were fired during a robbery. Someone died badly. Someone not involved. What had been a nickel-and-dimer graduated into a lifer.

I'd always kept a gun hidden on the seat of the car beside me. I hadn't ever pulled the trigger, I was the driver. But I had a gun.

The victim lingered, it took him a week to die. Murder. Kai'ea heard the news on the car radio, driving. We were killers. They'll be looking for us. He was alone; he pulled over to a stop, too dizzy to drive; the effect of the word murder nauseated him.

He broke with his partner; his girl disappeared. He got seriously ill with stomach pains, tried to recover, couldn't. There wasn't much left of him to arrest when the police finally got to him. He'd spent himself out.

The conscience his father had tried to push into him was somewhere in him still, even though I had put it to sleep. When it woke up, he was in the penitentiary, devastated. Inside, there was less prejudice, he earned respect the hard way. Too late.

Me. I am Kai'ea Porter, Hawaiian-Scotsman, a strong blend.

The first evening home in Waimanalo he wades out at Makapu'u, stands to his knees in sea water. He faces Manana Island, and 'way 'round over there, the Mokoluas. It is the cooling end of summer. The dash of waves on the rocks.

He stares out at Olomana Mountain, the sacred one. It begins to rain, a blessing. He sucks in the drenched air. I am home. I am Kai'ea Porter.

There were nights in the pen when this sound had spoken to him before sleep. All he can remember from the pen now are faces, faces, faces. Never tranquility. Friendships made under duress, always the clock, the calendar. When he arrived there, he was treated for ulcers. The first week someone broke his leg.

Over the years, he became obsessed with electronics, he studied year-old donated magazines. He read everything he could find on computer science. When a position in supply was announced, he took a test, passed, was given a job fixing computers.

Now he feels that he only brings detritus home with him, wiping his feet will not be enough. I carry years.

But I will try. I will present myself, walk into an office and ask for a job fixing computers. In one week.

It'll take him that long, a week, to build himself up into a man who believes he is needed, a man wearing new shoes, a man who can say no, and ask why. I will ransom my future for this job.

I walk to the store. I eat *poki* for the first time since I was sixteen. People I've never seen smile, ask about Mama. They greet me, Kai'ea, I wonder what they want. Then I know, I had forgotten, we're all in this together.

Tonight there is a moon; he pushes his bed under the window, lies where he can see his tree, its swords, silver, turning under the moon chrome, the breeze sizzling through the fronds. In the dark he feel the pain makua kane must have felt, his

Mama's pain for a son lost to her. He falls asleep listening to chickens settling down somewhere near.

At dawn, a rooster barks a broken cock-a-doodle-do to the new sun, its larynx stabbed by too many beaks. He lies in bed, knowing that he is not in jail. The dogs talk back and forth; the pig is busy next door. I hear a woman singing.

Looking up at his tree, I know it is all I have left of my island, makua kane.

Waimanalo. He feels close to something; he doesn't know what, in touch, maybe, with possibility. It is a mythological place, the deep growing flatlands that run from the pale beach to the base of the high furrowed cliffs. He looks up to the Ko'olau Mountains, feels his strength rise, feels the current, feels the healing begin. He is in contact with what matters, his island, the new day; he is available.

That morning, tutu from across the road remembers him as a boy, tells him she will cook for him.

He goes to visit Mama at the hospital. He has no money, strange clothes. The bus ride is ninety minutes. He's bewildered by the downtown he sees passing his window; Honolulu wants to be Seattle, Dallas, Los Angeles. No one else on the bus notices. He looks for Aloha Tower, his old landmark, but it is not there.

You are an island, be an island; makua kane said it is a blessing to be an island; be your own island; don't be afraid to be yourself. Be what you always were, unique.

Mama's face is lovely; when she hears his voice, her lips flatten against her teeth. It has been twenty-four years. She is breakable, smaller, calm. He touches her; she has no heat; her hands are tiny crabs. He cannot understand what she is trying to tell him. The stroke has cut vessels behind her eyes and now she is nearly blind. When he stands off to one side she can see him.

Her arm is like glass; there is nothing there.

The doctor tells him, she is not well enough to come home to Waimanalo after all. That was an agreement of his parole; he would come home and support her, but he is not a nurse. When his parole hearing came up for review, he was in good standing; his counselor talked to the board about his family crisis; the deal he made helped him win his release. Someone from O'ahu wrote a note to him in jail, If you had been here when your makua kane died, your Mama would never have had a stroke. The note was unsigned.

Thank you.

Kai'ea will visit Mama again tomorrow. But standing under his tree, he already knows. Well, niu, Mama's not ever coming home again.

Next morning he carries his old board to Makapu'u, to see what the waves are like. He wears beach shorts he's found in a drawer, no shirt. His board floats but he's heavy for it. The boards he sees around him in the sand are elegant, frivolous, but the surfers are serious, they wear the logotypes of corporations, matching tops. He sees money close to surfing.

His board is wizened; the glass had crazed; he has taped over the jagged skeg. I am the same; I have dozens of grey hairs, convict eyes.

A local guy, a huge moke walks over, calls him Pop. Kai'ea senses danger from him, turns to face him, squared off; he is in the prison yard again.

Do you know who I am, boy?

The moke tells him he sure doesn't.

I am Kai'ea Porter.

While the moke is forming a smile, Kai'ea leaps to his left side and knocks the legs out from under him. He has hardly touched him. He looks down at the moke.

Let's not have any more confusion about my name. The moke is smiling, he nods. Kai'ea gives him a hand up.

No one else makes him feel bad about his old board; no one crowds him in the lineup outside the wave break. He studies the break too long, sucks it all into his knees, gets up on a long ride. He can do it; they can tell. Maybe he used to be somebody, what do they know? Maybe a legend from Sa'moa,

From the shore someone yells, Shark!

Kai'ea glimpses the fin. Tiger shark. A dozen of surfers swim together; they form a pod as if they had rehearsed an aquabatics routine. Sharks do not attack massed surfers.

The shark has bitten a sixteen-inch crescent out of a board as if it were eating a waffle. Kai'ea's on the beach by then; he sees the kid swim in, trying to look cool, but when he tries to walk up the beach, he has fear cramps everywhere. Kai'ea sees the board, the kid; no one is hurt.

A photograph in the newspaper the next day, kid and board; he's a tourist from Japan. The editorial cries for relief from the shark menace. Tourism compromised. Small boat captains bait shark hooks; face the open horizon ready to clear the sea of sharks. A mission. Each day for a week, the biggest shark caught gets its carcass photographed alongside its vanquisher.

If the u'au kani pecks a hole in my surfboard, will they clear the sky of sea birds?

That night in the moon Kai'ea goes outside, whispers to his tree. Quick, give me an idea; I need your help. Is it too late to make Mama see some good in Kai'ea Porter? He knows that a coconut tree is not where you go to learn the answers; it is not full of ideas. He falls asleep, his head against the tree his arm on the root.

He wakes up. It is windy. In the dark, he sees it. A brief glimpse, nothing more, He doesn't need a longer look. He rolls over onto his feet, goes into the house, paces his boyhood room, thinking the idea through. He finds a pad and a pen. He has night eyes, he has gotten good at moving in the dark, writing. By the time he falls asleep again; it is all there.

In the morning, he wakes with his idea in his gut and it is still good. When he opens his eyes, there is his niu, its fingers combing the wind straight. A beautiful ache shoots through him down to his toes.

Good morning, niu. I, Kai'ea Porter, have good news.

His idea, an invention, has come without gestation. It is all there: an electronic device implanted in the body of a surfboard that emits the piercing whistle made by the shark's only natural enemy, the killer whale, the only creature it fears. Its sweeping cry will force the shark to swim the surfer by, to pass silently below, to dive, to disappear, to move along, to look elsewhere. It is as simple as that. It will force sharks away from surfers.

Kai'ea sees it. The device is small as a worn piece of soap, almost as thin as a watch, five ounces, with two AA batteries. He can build it.

Thank you, Niu. Kai'ea Porter is going to be a success; he's going to make his Mama and fadah proud. He talks to his tree. Talking to his tree is not deeply satisfying, but it is all he has of his island.

He knows about patents; he knows he needs to find a patent lawyer. For years he has read all the science magazines he could find, in them, stories of ripped-off scientists who sold their inventions for lunch money then watched the company sell them to the government for millions. Kai'ea needs to build his prototype.

Strange. This morning at the coffee shop, a man is sitting outside feeding birds, talking to them. Kai'ea knows that he needs to meet him. He introduces himself.

The man is not young. Kai'ea asks him what he was saying to the birds. The man smiles, he tells him he was talking to himself, that he just puts a bird in front of him to make it look better. Paul Marks is a lawyer, retired, relaxed. He is a hiker.

I am Kai'ea Porter, he tells him, I have an invention. Paul Marks laughs. Kai'ea tells him where he's been all these years. I am going to be a success. Paul Marks is amused by him, maybe uneasy. But he likes his story, his wide face, his suspicious eyes, his honesty. He does not take him seriously.

But when he hears Kai'ea describe his device, when he watches him sketch it out on the formica tabletop – the metal wafer backed by a piezo electric quartz wafer, the ultrasonic transducer, the emitter adapted to produce an ultrasonic to sonic sweep of sound – when he hears him imitate the sonar squeal of the whale that his little gadget will emit; he knows. He knows Kia'ea Porter's the real thing; he's been around; he knows who to believe in.

The next morning he meets Paul Marks at the coffee shop. He loans him seed money to build his prototype. He believes in him. He defers his fee, and applies for a copyright to protect the device from imitators. He tells him he needs a working name to put on the patent application.

Kai'ea takes a paper napkin and writes the words, Shark Off! Paul Marks likes it. "So will the surfers," he laughs. So it is named, Shark Off! He is proud of his invention, so is Paul Marks. We're so different, and we're friends.

Paul Marks makes things happen quickly; he's already registered his sketch of the surfboard implant at the patent office in Washington. In addition to the implant, Kai'ea has drawn a model that can be carried in the pocket of swimming trunks. There is a Shark Off! belt for swimmers of all sizes, for all ages. It will come in four colors.

With the patent, Paul Marks faxes the design proposal simultaneously to nine companies, giving them a three-week deadline to bid. The bidding is flashy; Australia's Bongo Boards answers Paul Marks' auction with the best bid, an offer he cannot refuse. They will market it for twenty dollars. Paul Marks retains a percentage of gross sales in Kai'ea's name, to be computed quarterly. He takes his fee, finally, a reasonable one, and with his initial advance payment, Kai'ea pays him what he owes. That feels very good.

I am Kai'ea Porter. I am rich. It has taken eleven weeks. He buys a set of tires for his truck.

He visits Mama, she is all the same, or less, she has been moved to a nursing home, Saffron Hill near Kaneohe.

When he tell her what he has accomplished, she doesn't understand. He tries to tell her again. Finally, she does, she grips his hand a long time, until he feels tears rise.

I never cried since I was a baby.

He tells Mama he's going to tell makua kane the news, she squeezes his hand again. That evening he goes to his niu.

I am a success, Niu, thank you. I know makua kane is listening. It is the best day of his life. He buys a foreign suit at Ala Moana shopping center.

Paul Marks advises Kai'ea to invest in property at once, he knows of a house on KoKo Head, a rich neighborhood. Good. I will better myself. The house is not yet on the market; he will buy it from a desperate couple, divorcing in a rage. The real estate lady is from Oregon, she has a powerful perfume and wears heavy gold objects. She brings a kahuna to bless the new house.

She lowers the selling price of Kai'ea's old family house and sells it in ten days. He says goodbye to his Niu. I will never forget you, Niu. I will come back to you.

Kai'ea moves from the sunrise side of the island to the sunset side. He packs everything he owns in his pickup truck. He drives only once, from Waimanalo to his new neighborhood, Koko Head. It is fourteen miles around Makapu'u, but it takes a thousand years.

At Waimanalo, the Ko'olau Mountains hang breathlessly where they were thrown high, two million years ago, turned into stone in mid-flight. They pose, now and forever; dangerous, sharp, fixed as they were when the lava cooled, a tableau for the sun and rain to describe.

Rounding Makapu'u, the Ko'olaus change. Fantastic on the sunrise side, they become rubble on the sunset side, piled in a lewd descent to the sea.

In the hills across from his new neighborhood, are villages of houses that look the same, all recently built on eminences and in crevices. Neat villages without stores or churches that stay lit all night long. Villages that have names like the titles of romance novels. Mariner's Ridge, Mariner's Cove.

His new house is on a cul-de-sac, quiet. It is wood and masonry; the roof is solid; everything works; there are washers and televisions; it is all new, decorated by the enraged couple who left behind their comfortable furniture, mostly white. From his lanai he sees across Maunalua Bay five miles to Diamond Head. He asks Mama's doctor, When will she be able to come and stay in my new house?

In his early years on O'ahu, he never saw the sun set over the ocean. He's only lived on the morning side of the mountains where the sun rises. He is well acquainted with the dawn, not with the sunset. Now, it is an endless spectacle for him.

Now he looks at the faceline of the Ko'olau Mountains. It is as though he has never seen them before. The bay below him has no Mokolua Islands, no uau kani, no Rabbit Island, no Chinaman's Hat, no destinations, nothing in Maunaloa Bay but a reef. But where there have been no eruptions there can be no islands to catch the birds, the sun. Here, on this side, it hardly ever rains on his street; the wind blows offshore, toward Sa'moa. The houses are like glass churches.

I am rich. I am Kai'ea Porter.

When he spots one of his new neighbors across the street he or she is usually turned away and cannot see Kai'ea wave hello. One neighbor always looks down; he is impressed by the effort she makes; but when he catches her eye she waves back vivaciously.

One morning he finds a parking ticket on his truck under the windshield wiper. In front of my house. There is no sign posted. None of his new neighbors had warned him.

A newsletter in his mailbox asks him to join the Neighbors Association, it tells him that this is a valuable part of Hawaii. I am rich, I live in an exclusive neighborhood where we need to protect what we own.

He cuts down a spiky plant; a neighbor watches him then says that it is an expensive plant.

The neighborhood security patrol driving by asks me who I am, for my own protection, one of them says politely. They are an old couple.

I am Kai'ea Porter. Who are you.

Oh, we're from Michigan. My wife and I.

They are from everywhere but here. You can move to New York and become a New Yorker, you can become a Texan, a Californian. But you cannot become a Hawaiian by moving here because you will never be Hawaiian. It is the only state where it is that way. They did not kill enough Hawaiian people.

He is not sleeping well, he turns, chained to his bed by memories. He turns, he sees his Niu in his dreams. He feel its absence, how a man who has lost a leg feels phantom limb pain. I cannot see the moon, there is an all-night yellow lamp stronger than the stars made of aluminum skeletons standing above our safe barren street.

There is no rooster to wake up to. At eight in the morning begins continuous noise. He watches from a window.

A man on the sidewalk with a gas engine strapped to his back blows bursts of dust up from cracks. But dust belongs in the cracks. At first he smiles, it is silly, curious to see a man with a machine loud as a chain saw blast little leaves. Leaves should be swept. Now he can tell the day of the week by which house is blasting its little leaves away.

I have been gone a long time.

Today a second letter comes from the Neighbors Association; it needs money for its legal fund so it may sue errant neighbors. One percent of my tax. A fair price, considering. The letter reads; "We have paid for higher standards, ours is a superior neighborhood."

But I cannot raise chickens or pigs here, or fix my pickup truck in the driveway, or keep my fishing boat in the yard, or build me a windmill, or hang my laundry out in the sun.

He shows the letter to Paul Marks who laughs at him, You've moved into litigation lawyer's paradise, Kai'ea.

Sometimes he walks his sidewalk in the mornings, looking up and down at the houses, high sharp angles.

Ugly. Nothing seems to belong here. I see nothing built by visitors on my island that is beautiful, that is worth looking at.

On his walk, slow runners pass him, stumbling forward grim-faced, wearing bright outfits. He sees despair in their faces, illness. Marching women in headsets pass him, punching their elbows high in anger. They nod seriously at each other. I have been away too long. Doesn't anybody go for a stroll anymore?

Mama once told him that the day he was born, when makua kane planted his tree, he placed a he'e, an octopus, into the puka under its young roots, so that its tentacles would show the roots how to reach out and grab the soil. A very old tradition.

I will bring my niu here to live with me. Why not? I am rich. I am Kai'ea Porter.

He calls Hawaii Hauling, the man says, No problemo, Mr. Kai'ea Porter. He picks a spot on his land below the house, digs a puka three feet wide and three feet deep, waits for his niu. He buys a small he'e from a fisherman, puts it in his freezer. On a Wednesday morning he drives to Waimanalo to watch the crew dig up his niu and lay it on a truck the size of a cruise ship. When it arrives at his new property, there is a problem, it needs to be carried in backwards. When they lower the roots into the *puka* on top of the *he'e,* they swing it in its place, turning it west and south, facing it away from the trade winds, as if it has always lived here. The neighbors are not visible, but he senses movement behind shades, silent concern. The job takes all day until evening.

In the dark, he stands in his kitchen, the wind drives the house forward through the night, a bag settles in the garbage, a long-dead lunatic trapped under the house scratches the windowsill. I have my niu.

"Mr. Kai'ea Porter, your tree is in violation of Obstruction Code Ten." A typewritten note on Neighbors Association stationery, written in a pleasing neighborly tone. Unsigned, a committee letter. Kai'ea Porter, it suggests, has thirty days to comply with this program: "Kindly top the tree by ten feet, at your convenience, or remove it entirely from your property."

A week passes. With his niu closeby, he sleeps better, sometimes he sleep outdoors on the grass where he can wake to it under the moon. But his tree has gone into deep shock, for two weeks it barely survives, it drops fronds. There is more sun on this side of the island, more wind, rocky volcanic soil. But the he'e grips the soil and its roots spread. Without a word, his niu teaches him that because something depends on you, don't think a debt needs to be paid.

Another notice comes in the mailbox from the Neighbors Association, unsigned. "Your coconut palm tree is compromising several views, it devalues properties."

How can my tree compromise a view? My tree is the view. My niu is beautiful.

The note continues, "Remove it immediately or the Neighbors Association will take measures to do so."

I am Kai'ea Porter. Who are these people? If I am rich, why am I living here? Where is Hawaii? There is no room left in Hawaii for Hawaii.

When I was a baby, Mama held up this globe of the world for me to see; she pointed out our islands. I couldn't imagine that they were really where we lived. For one thing, the islands were tiny, all by themselves out there in the middle of nothing. For another thing, our chain of islands resembled droppings of an unwell, traveling dog. How could we live on these droppings of land, when there are big places, South America and Australia, Russia, Africa? I cried, tears ran from my eyes for a long time that night.

The next day, makua kane carried me on his shoulders to the top of the sacred mountain, Olo'mana. The two of us sat looking out over our island and we talked about everything. While we sat there, the weather changed three times.

When we came down that afternoon, I knew that we were not born on our island by mistake, that no one is ever born anywhere by mistake. Makua kane told me that I was unique, that each one of us on these islands is unique.

He told me: You will come across people from those bigger places who have come to our island to change the way things are. That is how they spend their lives. And they will change the way things are, too, but they must never change the way you are, Kai'ea.

You will go your own way, you will come to each adventure and learn, you will try hard, you will make your stay on our island important because you will remain yourself.

But I warn you, Kai'ea. These are formless people who have come to our island. They were never happy where they were living. That is why they are here, and they will bring the reasons they were never happy with them.

I don't know why I wake up, there is no reason.

A concussion in the air? It comes from outside.

Through his window the moon is kindling the housetops down to the bay. A night of magic, lit by the bright soullessness of the moon. The moon itself is gaunt. Tree shadows more distinct than their sources.

There it is again. Nothing more than an impression.

I go outside naked. I look over my land.

And my niu. I cannot see it; the moon is in my face. I walk toward my niu. I look for my niu. I am moonblind. I stand at where it is. I cannot see it. It has been cut down. There is only a stump. My niu is gone.

The blood drains from his mind; he is pale with anger, he whispers, I am Kai'ea Porter. Then he cries in a rage, to wake the neighborhood, I am Kai'ea Porter.

EX LIBRIS

ॐॐ

Me? I am Auguste Banat. I have never known why my dead mother named me so. August. I was born in November. A strange woman, my mother, she might have intended to imply greatness upon me from Augustus Caesar, after all, still, a heavy load for a small child. I am told I became quite trying at the dinner table, children named after adjectives will only try to live up to them.

I am certainly not a great man. I prospered and for years was able to enjoy the fruits from my various trees. Throughout my lifetime, I simply did to others as they would have done to me a moment or two before they would have done it. Ethics? Without the word unethical enterprise would cease to exist. As you already know, if you want to make a bouillabaisse, you need to kill fish. Certainly business would no longer have amused me and perforce I would have reverted to ordinary labor such as farming.

I had a family once; now I am alone. My two children have better things to occupy themselves with than to visit their old father. Their lives complicated by choices. And wasn't I the same when I was their age?

This may be more than you would care to know about me; I beg your pardon; I did not see you come in; I would not be speaking to you in this manner unless I felt it was urgent to do so.

In the Midi, in the Auvergne between Aurillac and Tulle at a large rough stone farmhouse, a man named Auguste Banat mumbles to himself; he stands mumbling before his bookshelves in the library room that was attached to the farmhouse end of the last century. In that dark stone room shaped by the raw beams overhead, the stone floor underfoot, the blackened hearth, the Medieval tapestry "The Duke's Hunt," a crowd of books on the shelves stand waiting for him to speak.

Though it is a bright morning on the hillside, fresh and clear outdoors, it is still dark in this room. The small deep-set window like a pig's eye, handles the sunlight without courtesy and allows only a single ray to muscle its way in.

Evenings after a dinner cooked by Mme Matthias, Auguste Banat will stand in front of these books holding a glass without ice half-filled with fluid the color of wild honey; perhaps it is single malt whiskey from Scotland, an Irish whiskey or possibly a Cognac from the district near Bordeaux.

Auguste loves his books to distraction, certainly as much as he loves his glass. It was once his habit to buy armloads of books along the Paris quais to be read at some non-existent future date, and there they wait, some for years unopened, waiting for him, and, he feels, true and loyal.

He stands in front of his shelves, drifting from friend to friend. Here he has many friends, some new, some old. Some unmet. Ingenious, reliable, trusted and wise, they are his only friends. He has no one left outside this room. He has either forsaken or been forsaken by them. He is an incomplete man devoid of raisons d'être. He has nothing.

We begin with simplicity, we struggle for a lifetime and if we achieve success, we attain simplicity.

He recognizes certain books by their bindings of course, as acquaintances, somewhat as you would a lady encountered at a dinner whose name you have forgotten, those books he had scarcely met and looks forward to knowing.

But it is his old friends he habitually pulls down when the fire has aged and he stands on the layers of rugs in his socks, with his Cognac, his cigar. These are the friends he has lived with, those he has come to treasure, to rely upon in his long nights' solace. To fill his great sadness. And of course Aug- uste has more friends standing before him than he has in the world beyond this room in this stone house in the Auvergne.

These are the faces I love. Smart people entre-scene at the Paris opera, the Comedie, dining at the finest restaurants, those who while away the blue hours at cafes, the ones I used to greet at Longchamps in the spring, those who think and argue, fascinating or dull, people worth distinguishing.

His friends no longer come around. Of course, why should they? His sons and daughter resent him. They believe he should have been jailed for his business practices. His own family.

Family. It is nothing more than a small group of strangers and pickpockets trapped in the Metro for life.

The death of Marie. When my wife died I left Paris for good. My children were grown. I chose the Auvergne. I discovered this farm house; it was already named Le Morne des Betes, the hill of animals; I kept the name and bought goats and sheep. A year went by, then another. I longed for a companion. My idea of a woman was one who only wanted isolation, who was ready for it, whom I could read aloud to or she to me, sit beside, turn pages over the long evening in the old fire lit room, our lamps lit, sipping from glasses, a cold bottle of champagne on a table between us. A woman of beauty who did not mind cigar smoke, who understood its aroma. A romantic woman to whom money had the power to buy nothing worthwhile except isolation. I sought this woman and so I traveled to Paris Lyons Nice north to Brussels then up to Sweden, vaguely searching for this woman in cafes, restaurants, museums. How does one search for love? I had not expected to find love again; I only hoped to find friendship. Of course, I was a trace too serious. There was perhaps too much quietude in me for a young woman.

But no. I found Aureole in of all places while I was dining outdoors down by the docks in Bastia the old capital of Corsica.

Aureole. I knew. In two days I felt the delightful fear of falling from a great height and not caring if I would land safely or not. I was in love. With Aureole, I was more deeply in love than I had thought possible; it was the stuff of bilious romance novels. I now can truly believe that every man who is as lucky as I had been, remains a virgin until he finds his final love. And Aureole was mine.

She traveled back with me to Le Morne des Betes. We took a car from Nice. I was quite apprehensive, but to my surprise she adored the house the farm the grounds. I introduced her to Monsieur et Madame Matthias, the caretakers. I introduced her to my books.

We were married immediately in the village by the priest and the mayor. The village turned out for the wedding; everyone drank and danced. No one was excluded of course. It was there at the wedding feast that I met Pierrot Fleury. I thought I had quickly forgotten him. But I did remember his dishonest eyes, grey eyes, and that he spoke not above a whisper. We drove to Barcelona for our honeymoon, toward Barcelona actually, because we never arrived; we stopped at nameless fishing villages along the Catalonian coast and listened through the night to the great sadness of their flamenco. I never knew playing dominoes could be exciting. Our month was gone we turned for home.

For the next two years Aureole and I shared a dreamlike life of dual solitude away from the complicated world, in the ancient French countryside. We ate and drank well, we sang and we danced, we grew herbs, harvested lavender and grapes, we worked our land, and we read books aloud to each other made love and slept soundly. Sometimes we traveled but never far, never to America or China for example. Together we lived two years of sweat and stars, two years of song.

Aureole left him for another man.

A thief. My life was over once again, this time for good. It was now worse than being a widower. Death is an act of God. Betrayal is an act of humanity. It was the one from the wedding.

He had been without a centime when he came to my door asking for work. At the time, I needed a chauffeur, a handy man, an errand runner. He had been told how to find my house in the village. Pierrot Fleury. All that he had to offer me was a curiously distinguished profile, a head you see on coins. I would not have doubted him if he had claimed to be descended from the house Bourbon. But he only hinted at royal ancestry. Anyhow, he seemed too clever to be in the plight he appeared to be in. He seemed too clever for the jobs I gave him. And a lazy man's ability to invent shortcuts to make his life easier. He acted humbly to me, of course. As for his humility, in his case it was the hiding place of egotism, malice pride, arrogance. He had long fingers and fingernails. At first he did not seem entirely masc- uline. As it turned out he was, of course, but for the time he was here, and he was cleverer than his employer. He poured from my best bottles too freely, as a guest might pour who has never been a host. He resembled the sort of man who needed to be cradled by a woman. Soon enough, my wife Auréole obliged him.

One spring morning she came to me and asked if she might go to Paris to visit the galleries and buy paintings for the house as a surprise for me she would redecorate it while I was away on a trip to Lyons. I was delighted to say yes. I admired her taste. It was arranged that she would fly to Paris and buy her artwork and whatever else she wanted and Pierrot would drive the truck to Paris a week later and pick up the paintings and sculptures and bring them back to Le Morne des Betes.

I left on my trip to Lyons.

While I was away they vanished. Without a trace.

Of course the artwork was lost. It was a simple plan of rob-bery. They joined the paintings and sculptures wherever they had shipped them.

I wanted him tortured and would have killed him on sight with pistol or sword. Of course he knew that. I attempted to find them but was only able to follow the art to Zurich; their trail vaporized in Switzerland. The art meant nothing to me of course, five million francs.

Naively I had believed that there can be absolutely no connection between love and money, and if there were, well, there could be no love.

I am alone, I have already told you that. I did not kill myself; suicide has always been out of the question, I am of Basque origin. I stayed alive only in the hope of revenge.

The old woman, Mme Matthias continued to cook the brutal cuisine of the south, with olives and capers and garlic and anchovies. Madame Matthias and her husband Monsieur were both full of slumber, which was fine with me; not many tasks needed to be attended to at the farm.

I never considered seeking yet another woman to fill the other half my bed, my conversations, my life, to sit across me at my table. I never sought her. That part of my life was over. All that was left to me was a hopeless quest of revenge. I talked to myself frequently, why not, and so did they, the Matthiases, so between all of us talking to ourselves there was a good deal of talk in the house. I simply could not resign my life to sadness. I needed my books above all else. Books more than ever before became the great and only stabilizer left in my life. Where my world had turned against me, my books stood by me.

On those hundreds of open-eyed nights when I finally surrendered, and got up, stood by my bed, dry with sleeplessness, I could feel my books waiting; I could hear them when they spoke to me. I did not ever look at the clock. One book would ask to be taken down and opened. I could hear the voice of another book, familiar, speaking, then another. I would draw them from the shelf and sit under the good iron lamp usually with a cigar, an ounce or two without ice, and become engulfed. It was a good, maybe a strange thing, but I clearly heard their voices, the voices of the characters within them speaking to me. I could easily imagine where each chapter may have been written, whether indoors or out, in what season, in what mood, and at what time of day. At a bench under a tree? Above an ocean? At a table before a window. Indoors. There must always be a window indoors.

On certain nights, I felt the fullest force of the titles shouting at me from the shelves, so much thought, so many years of ideas, so many passions at work and at play. I became confused, those nights; I could not escape the room; I felt full madness and I poured myself to sleep.

Am I talking too much?

Oh, maybe so.

Auguste never left his property any more, never went into the village. It was only his books. The cinemas and television were useless; they had all done their work. Was he losing his mind? A possibility. On all those restive nights that he'd stood spellbound before his books and listened to their voices, he told no one of his madness. Who was there to tell that he was constantly haunted by loss, knowing that Aureole was somewhere at that exact moment possibly touching Pierrot in her beautiful sleep.

She was somewhere with him in the world. Who was there to tell? Monsieur and Madame were already half mad.

Then a coincidence.

Auguste received a telephone call from a man he had to university with, a friend from Paris, a stamp collector, a dilettante archaeologist. This man swore to Auguste that he had seen a woman he believed to be his wife on a tiny Greek island named Sires. In its only harbor, this woman had been seated alone, a glass of coffee and a liqueur. The cafe was near the fishing boats.

The man had no idea that Aureole had left Auguste, and he was just about to walk over and introduce himself (I mean what a coincidence after all), when a handsome man sat down beside her and kissed her. He watched them at a distance, talking. Her hair was short, but it could have been no one else, he told Auguste; she had her distinct look, that high bridged nose, the long elegant face, those strangely shadowed eyes. Impossible but there it was. Auguste questioned him about the man. Very much hair, grey eyes. He could be nobody but Pierrot. What else?, Auguste asked him. Sadly, the man said, I can only report that they seemed quite happy.

What was I supposed to do? Let them be? Let them live? The trail was simple to follow and of course I would follow it. They never would know it. Before I left for Greece, I found a book that had fallen behind her bedtable. A book she had forgotten with a map of the Greek islands; there was the same island, Sires, circled with her pen, the island of their dreams.

I hardly remember traveling to Greece, then Arkos, then to an even smaller island, Sires. I had to cross to the island aboard the water barge on its weekly trip. The water company gave me their address. There was no hotel in Sires; I took a room with a fisherman's family. For the next three days I lived in a trance; I tasted no food; I only saw pictures of what I was seeing; my head was constantly ringing.

My once beloved Aureole and this item, Pierrot, lived in a stone house above a rocky ledge, dangerously close to the sea below. A pretty plastered house, not large. They seemed to have kept some money; there was a fishing boat that appeared to be theirs. They had no telephone of course. It all seemed very romantic. No complications. I watched them with binoculars. It seemed quite natural what I was doing, so right. I rather enjoyed the thrilling pain of watching their silly lives at a distance as if they were miniature puppets and I were holding their strings. I was, of course. By then I had made an exquisite plan.

The sweet pain of knowing was constant, excruciating during the black nights. But the thought of what I planned to do to them made it possible to survive. I only had to stay on that damned island four days, until the mailboat came.

Once-a-week at their house, they took delivery of water in five litre bottles.

The day I was leaving for the mainland, the fisherman's wife asked me if I knew the French couple with the house over- looking the sea.

"Why no," I said, "why?"

"Well, they will die."

"Was it the water?"

"No, no, no. The water is good. We all drink the same water."

The dreadful rumor was that Aureole and Pierrot had been taken ill together, poisoned by the same tainted fish. I could see them lying together in bed at Death's door. It was my suspicion that they were not dying of poisoning but from badly tainted water. I gave the woman a few drachma and a stamped envelope addressed to me. I asked her to write me of any rumors she might hear of their demise.

"Will they bury them here on Sires?" I asked. I don't know why I cared.

"A boat will come from the mainland to take them to a hospital at Athens."

As I stepped aboard I felt immensely relieved. Even if one does somehow survive yellowfish poisoning, one's brain never quite recovers.

Back at Le Morne des Betes, I slept through the nights again without the help of my decanters for the first time in two years.

It was nearly ten days before the woman's letter arrived. Her husband had assured her that neither had survived. Their house was pillaged, of course, it is the custom on those poor islands. And the woman went on to describe a locket that I had once given Aureole with a tiny photograph inside. That person resembled me she wrote. There were no hospital records and no one I asked could ever find their graves.

At night late he still went to his shelves to seek out a book. There it was, near the shelves on a small table he never used.

Maybe I had once bought that book, who knows? But if I had I was not aware of it; I had never seen this book before.

It charged me to pick it up. It wasn't what I had imagined, a colorful book, well-bound. No, this book was bound in soft cloth, cream colored. There was nothing to distinguish it, no words written on the outside, no title, no publisher, nothing. Inside, the author's name and one word, Tales.

Immediately, I was drawn to this book. It was full of stories. I read two or three that night before falling asleep. All I can remember about them was that they were calm, simple short and well written and when I put the book down I felt closer to my life. They had been written in an extended weary sigh, maybe one of remorse.

The pages had not been numbered. Rare but not unheard of. Only odd. The book might have been published anytime in the past few decades. The author might have been English French Greek. André Prosody. He had either never lived or was dead as far as I knew, and the publishing house, once in Lyons, no longer existed according to the directory.

The next day I had a strange thought, that the Tales in the book were trying to remark on my life, to smile at me. What it contained was nothing more than narratives of people I'd never met of course, but people of my stratum I might have known in another place, sophisticated people of rank with certain advantages. People who had gotten where they had by artful means, who had clawed and gouged and even killed who had done what was required to succeed. Arrived people who mattered. It seemed a savage thought, but I could not ignore it.

Of course that dreamlike line running through the Tales that reminded Auguste of his own sins, was told by someone who knew him quite well, from another world a safe distance away. The Tales left Auguste with an ugly restiveness, as if he had imbibed a literary arsenic. But it was a caste that carried him back to the book again and again.

Was I imagining this? That these Tales actually preyed upon my being? It seemed so. But I wasn't to blame. I was no more immoral than the rest. Maybe I had destroyed a few people in my lifetime, but I had needed to. Maybe I had killed wife and her lover.

One night he wanted to find a story that he had read before, a story that reminded him of an incident in his past. He couldn't find it. The story was not there. He'd had a few malt whiskeys and he was able to convince himself that he was wrong. He must have made a mistake.

But when it happened again the next night, another story gone, he put his glass down. Then it happened a third night. Something was very wrong.

They simply were not there. Was I losing my mind? Was the book losing its stories? Whichever it was hardly mattered. Is this a new form of madness? Was this a door slightly opened to my life that suddenly slammed shut?

And the stories began to change. They turned darker, they ended badly. The book became leaner. One by one the stories were disappearing from the book.

I could no longer go back and find any story that I had read in the book. But the book called to me; then one night, you must believe me; I heard it scream my name. I grabbed it and held it in my hand.

He held the book a long time. It had become very lean. And his hands trembled as he poured himself a glass and sat down in his leather chair. Finally he opened it. There was only one story left. It told of a man who loved his books who traveled to a tiny Mediterranean island. The man was named Auguste Banat. When he got to this island he poisoned a beautiful woman and her lover, Pierrot Fleury. But he did not succeed. They lived. And when they recovered, they came back to visit Auguste.

This is how we found him, sitting in his leather chair, this empty book in his hand. He is unable to speak. He cannot move. He can only stare at me.

Who am I? I am Pierrot Fleury.

Gardner McKay

THE MAN WHO FORGOT TO DIE

୬ೕ

5:20 a.m.

Outside, he listens to the first bus of the day catch gears and climb the slope, slow down at the bus stop, the hot sigh of air brakes. The next bus will be along in twelve minutes.

The bastion of small storefronts still sleeps in the mist that surrounds this part of Brooklyn. He lies in the pale room, waiting for six buses to slow and stop, for each gasp of air brakes. In the thick window light, he watches the room gradually become a museum of familiar artifacts, famous only to him. The day already seems unimportant, already finished. Only the bed sheets, thin with age, feel friendly to him.

When the six buses have passed by, he rises and moves in darkness, eyes closed, barefoot across his warren, blind, toward the stove to heat water for coffee, to locate and toast bread. To the mirror, to confirm that an extra thumb has not grown out of his forehead in the night. To the chill of the bathroom floor and the gaily flickering fluorescent death-lights, then shaving badly with the molten eyes of a problem drinker. The toilet's plumbing performs with familiar lethargy that to him seems personal; he reads his swirling droppings for signs of death, as if reading them might instruct him. The water he set on the stove screams; the toast has jumped high and dry. Life rises within him, defying oblivion. Homo sapiens urbanus, late 20th Century.

From the floor, he scoops up a page ripped from his spiral notebook. He un-crumples it and reads his handwriting, written in a continuous snarl, firm and clear from his late-night beliefs, the clotted dreams of a professional mourner; written with intense logic in place of creativity. And he reads his words in a snarl, rapidly mumbling the outline of a story no one will ever read voluntarily: We're all going to end up in jars, OK?, not the same size jars, some will be larger. From the beginning we're taught to look ahead toward these jars. Every day. Presumably safe, in an over-lit hospital bed, dead from natural decay or from a nasty plague – following over-priced days and nights with nose, arm, and kidney tubes. Or die more suddenly; the result of three a.m.lunacy. Or the normalcy of a plane crash, maybe a stray bullet. The unexpected death by our own hand, sedatives, falling, or driving your motorcycle into a copse of firs ...

He says aloud he will make it better. In motion now, with coffee and dry toast, back toward the bed he picks up a pair of undershorts, sniffs them, balls them and throws them into the bathtub with socks and shorts, finds another pair, rejects them, too. He dresses without interest like a little boy in yesterday's clothes, unaware of the colors, if any, he is wearing.

Below his window, two storeys down, a medieval jogger swims past, scraping the pavement, clawing the air, wincing. Nothing shows me death more clearly than an ancient jogger. He sets his coffee cup on the painted table-top and sits in the Shaker chair, suitable only for stacked boxes. No milk. He continues reading aloud from the crumpled page:

...or we can die from not living, from merely filling in the colors. Those who already know from an early age what they like and don't like, who they are, what they're going to do, who they will marry, where they will live, where they will die. With their knowledge comes the power to instantly bore whomever they meet. Except those with the same power, for they are clinically dead, only lacking toe-tags. They cannot be jump-started ...

"Oh, wise Lord, I can make that better." He sips his viscous carbon-black coffee, wincing. I've got to have milk.

He's known about her all summer long, living next door, seen her in glimpses, clean-limbed, clear-headed, smart, up-and

-away early; lovely Margaret. She is made of milk. But his timing, his depressions, his appearance, the transparent frames of his mind have never quite dovetailed into the right coincidence needed to meet her. She will give me milk from her body.

He knocks on her door.

He can hear her peering at him through the tiny lizard's eye in the door. She opens it fully to him, gives him a look to bisque a leopard. She is wearing a white half-slip, but tying a terry cloth robe over it. Her face is dripping, half-washed. He gasps. She's showing herself to me.

"I'm from next door."

"I know that, you're Martin. And I'm going to be late." She speaks to him as if they were already married. That she's been expecting him. Ten minutes ago.

"Sorry, really ... I hate to ... Look, do you have any milk?" He doesn't call her by name, although he's known her name all summer.

She sees his cup of black coffee and curls her mouth very nicely at the corners, a smile of ridicule. Do you have milk? Is this request ordinarily made of her? He hears the uneven tenor snarl of what must be a tiny dog, emanating from the corner behind her.

"That's Miguel," she said. A small movement of whiskers and feathered feet confirms life under a chair. "He's pretty feral. Better say hello, Miguel."

"Hello, Miguel." Miguel doesn't respond. A rat dressed for a football game.

"Do you really want milk?"

"Yes, of course, but if ... Look, I mean I can't drink this without cutting it ... " It resembles India ink.

She smiles, suddenly filling the room with herself.

"Please come in. Her robe falls away as she points to a small blue pitcher, "It's over there, see?" She reaches high on the bathroom door for a whitish dress that clings to a hanger. When she takes it down, she spins, and the door mirror briefly reflects the backs of her thighs. She lays the dress on the bedspread, measuring out her length in bed for him to imagine.

"Or was knocking on my door just ... curiosity?"

"No."

"Well, why, Martin, after three months, are you suddenly curious about meeting me? We could have met last May." She speaks to him with the familiarity of a wife.

"All summer long I was alone much too much, I think."

"I was working."

"Please tell me quickly, because I am definitely late." She's enjoying this.

"I'm not curious about you. I mean, I am curious, but not this morning. This morning I just want to be able to drink my coffee and make my head function so I can finish something I'm working on."

"Well, I've been curious about you, who wouldn't be? You're a character, so quiet and calm. You talk to yourself, you stay up late, you sing, you run every day. I felt it was OK having you next door, a runner, I knew I could pound on the wall if I ever needed help." While she talks, she smooths her dress on the bed.

"But you never needed help."

"No. Knock Jarman."

They both knock Jarman, he, mindlessly. She lets a silence fall between them. He is still standing in the doorway, unbelievably, open to the hallway.

"Please close it."

He does, a new rushing sound in his ears.

"Your name is Martin Jarman."

"Yes, officer." Not good enough. My name needs to be Adrian Hemisphere, Ernest Clarendon, Tarik Garance. Not Martin Jarman.

"I'm Margaret Ashenberg. Meg, please. What do you do?"

"What do I do," he answers lamely.

"Yes, I can't figure it out."

He's weary of hearing himself say what he does when he is not doing it well.

"Is it hard to explain?"

"No, not hard to explain. I'm just a writer. I write stories, fiction, you know," he says.

"That's good, no?"

"No. It used to be good years ago, being a writer, now it's nothing."

"Really?"

"Yeah." The New Yorker calls us chroniclers who gaze upon the world with youthful wonder. "You?"

"Oh. I work for an art book publisher called Ankram House," she nods to the west, toward Manhattan. "What's that?"

The crumpled page in his hand. "Something I wrote last night."

"May I hear it?"

Half in the bathroom, she slips the whitish dress over her head and smooths it to her shape while he reads the fragment quickly, not in a snarl, but in a whisper, as if it were a love poem.

" ... or that we die only because we don't live. We do not look into the corners of our lives, or down the corridor beyond, or out the window, across the park, the river, the city. Sometimes we try. We travel, and we pack our void with us. We see old civilizations, we breathe their air, we hurry home exalted, unable to change. Our regrets in life, then, are not the things we've done and failed at, but the things we simply haven't done at all. We are not living on Death Row, waiting to die. We are living on Life Row, waiting to come to life ... "

"That's lovely, Martin, it's deep and sad. Now I'm late." She is choosing earrings. "I'm trying to decide right now if I should call in and say I'll be in after lunch."

She has left several buttons open on her skirt, above the hem. She sits on the edge of the bed and as she sits, reveals a tiny flash of pure white, her inner thigh, the area high between her legs where they come together. She looks directly at him. "Can you help me make up my mind?"

He feels a continuous sound rushing in his ears and decides that it is his own blood.

"It's an hour's ride by subway; should I call?" She sits on the edge of the bed, her un-stockinged knees one or two inches apart. Her impatience is magnificent.

Now? Right now, with Margaret? He has studied her all summer long. He has listened for her to come home late afternoons, and later. Wondered about her. She has never had a visitor. And all those early July evenings when she left her door ajar to draw the cool breeze up the stairs through her apartment. All summer long.

He has pictured this moment quite differently. He has seen preludes involving lengthy but non-filling dinners of appetizers, the Museum of Modern Art, glistening wine, gradual revelations, time slowed to a standstill, a lone candle guttering in a saucer, Gregorian chants. He sets his cup on a low bureau with small-framed photographs of older people.

"Please, Martin, tell me what to do."

"Call in late."

With a nude arm, she reaches for the telephone.

Early that afternoon, as he glides away from her apartment in exultation, away from their building, Meg's and his building, nearly executed by a taxi as he crosses the street, he feels stronger and weaker, renewed, cleansed, historically confident and secretly sure, now holding his spiral notebook rolled in his hand, he crosses the street into the rich yellow sun of the park, fat with leaf-shade from the great bundles of trees; then onto the thick grass he walks below the leafed elbows of the elms and maples and he smells the air borne from the grass from a long day's sun – an ageless sunlight, strong on the greenswards where he goes forth, new from the largesse of a woman that until this morning he had only barely imagined to be possible.

He is brimming with ideas for a story, for a book, for a universe without hatred. He writes in his floppy spiral notebook: I will never, never be able to explain the awesome, simple tie connecting a man and a woman that is, at exactly the same moment, one million years old and still fresh on my penis.

Lying beside him, she has told him that he has a runner's body, a body of long planes, and that she has seen his body in a painting by Delacroix, as an archer. Later, at the end, she has confessed that once on an especially warm morning, she sat in a chair by her window and touched her clitoris until she came while watching him run back and forth through the park like a wolf.

"You actually masturbated while you were watching me run?"

"I never use that word."

"Latin, master, seed, tubari, to disturb," he continued gravely, stupidly, "To agitate the seed."

All summer long she has been there, a wall away, available to help him find cheap international restaurants, to shop for books with him and choose movies, to tell him all about her day, to listen his stories, his daily arrangements of words, to hoard Saturdays with him, to drink too much with him, to behave any way they want in bed, to fulfill his requests, to share their head-clearing morning-after breakfasts, to divide wine, laughter, biographies. All summer long, a wall away, a door ajar. Does time pass or do we pass time?

Now, today is her last day at Ankram House. Meg was not able tell him about Italy before he left her at midday. She's given up on New York. She's disillusioned, she's quit her job, found a replacement. She is moving to Florence to walk, to see, to learn a better life. After work, her office gives her a champagne toast and a book about Florence. In two days she's leaving the city for good.

He sits in the twilit park. He watches himself swirling from across the street. He feels victorious over an invisible foe and it doesn't matter that he knows no one he can tell who will understand. He feels young and old, just born and fully matured. Born in a park. He has finally met someone with the power to alter his course, to substitute meaning for meaningless. He has done it at last, he is free, and he has nowhere to go tonight that matters, nor tomorrow, and he truly doesn't care because his life, whatever it is, and wherever it is going, has just begun. He has found her. Close to his bench on the Green, stands that marvelous stupid ox, Love, staring at him with huge Italian eyes.

Now, reverentially in his spiral notebook, he begins to write the outline for his new novel, A Death in Brooklyn: About a writer who has bizarre impulses and carries them out to their conclusion. Each time, he can barely retrieve himself from his wild excursions. He acts without control from the same temperament that allows him to create as a genius. Should we condemn him? No, we should admire him; the value of his art outshines his transgressions.

That evening she cooks him a dinner of garlic soup and balsamic salad with fine strips of Parmesan cheese. Their first dinner. After midnight, when they are sitting in the dark listening to music, the ruminations of cello, she is able to tell him that she is leaving for Florence that weekend. She speaks to him with lightness. He feels a split-second stun-sound in his ears, then it passes. His despair is neutral. Come live with me in Florence.

That night the city flows beneath them almost without a sound. For a long time they sit naked across from each other and stare out the window at the street. The bulbs of the street lamps are cold in the breathless late-summer air. A door downstairs slams shut.

I write stories. I write about disengaged people who are dying of boredom but don't know it, or they think it's embarrassment. I write stories about people paralyzed by the system who can't get out, maddeningly attached to the surfaces of life. Stories about the emasculation of the species in our society.

Martin cannot possibly leave the city. His connections are here. There is his apartment, his writing; he has just this afternoon begun to work on a novel. He understands this city, is pathologically alert to its streets, to its gradual decay of progress. Distant acrid smoke, the scent of a stripped car burning. He reads The New York Times each morning searching for clues. All of his unwritten works sleep beneath him each night. He has cavities in his teeth. She leaves that weekend.

I run. I run a good four-mile course from Canarsie Boulevard to Flatbush Avenue and back up 116th Street. I run every day. My body is sacred. I want to live as long as I can. I see joggers running who'll outlive everyone they know but will be dead the whole time.

At the airport, she gives him a going-away present, a small book of poems; in it she writes her address in Florence. She has arranged to lease a flat near the Piazza del Appia. Martin will certainly write her long letters and tell her how his novel is coming along. They kiss. She is barefaced, a fugitive lock of her hair from the night before dangles between them. He watches tears film her eyes, and then she is gone.

He stands a moment looking after her, down the spiny corridor leading to her plane. To be beautiful at an airport is to be beautiful anywhere. He turns to go. It's still early. He will buy the Times and have a coffee, a special coffee today, a cappuccino at Il Dolce Cafe, two subway stops from his apartment.

Sitting in the cafe with the Times still folded, he holds his cappuccino between ten fingertips; he imagines Meg walking in Florence, a city to which he has never been. She is wearing a longish beige skirt, hurrying through a light rain under a clearing sky, holding a magazine over her hair. He imagines a young Italian who lives in her building near the Piazza del Appia, maybe on the floor below hers, her neighbor, watching her from his window.

He knows that the Italian gentleman has the courtliness of a doge, allows the young Italian half-an-hour to knock on her door, to offer her his services as a guide, to touch her hand.

ALL THAT MATTERS

But when I saw her, she was not running. She was looking my way, walking down the steps carefully, a dream. She didn't see me. Down the steps she came toward me, blankly, step by step, down the wide, granite steps of the Berne Clinique des Femmes. I didn't know until I touched her that was crying. We'd come to Switzerland, not intending to stay long, driving our way down from Norway down through Belgium and France to Italy. Our first honeymoon after nine years of marriage. We'd traveled a bit during those nine years, on working vacations, and we had worked well together, but this was to be our honeymoon. It had seemed like a good idea at the time, and long due.

Then she fell. That cool blue midday, on the field under the pines by the lake south of Geneva. She had been bringing napkins from the car. I had been sitting on the grass, unscrewing the vinyl cork from a bottle of gas station wine, and after she fell I watched her lying there in the short grass for a few moments, waiting for her to get up, but she didn't. I thought she'd decided to lie there seductively, looking up through the pines at the sky while I made romantic overtures. We'd been playing endless games on our honeymoon. So I stood up and made a couple of sexual suggestions to her in bad French, waxing an imaginary mous- tache. Everything seemed funny. We'd been playing these trashy games, acting like silent film lovers and laughing at ourselves for the first time in years.

She wasn't laughing. She didn't answer me right away. Eventually she said, "Help me." I was more confused than frightened.

And that is how all of this at the Berne Clinique got started.

The night we met, a sopping night nine years ago in Seattle,

I'd been unshaven for days and slightly drunk from a long visit to a bar that had just closed; my glasses were cloudy, my fingernails were dirty, and my old Burberry was soaked clear through. I'd been earning a so-so living as a writer, writing supermarket love stories under a woman's name. My late marriage had killed any desire to write anything more provocative, say, my novel, and with the recent death of that marriage had died any illusions, other than those magazine stories with the florid titles that would be cluttering my obituary. I had once tried to be a writer in a more meaningful tradition; why couldn't publishers have seen that? But no, like the public, that great snail, they asked for variations of past work.

Well after midnight, I'd walked in out of the drizzle into a supermarket, lit like an amusement park, and had paced the color-bright aisles leaving a dog's wet trail, staring at the few pale shoppers, studying the regiments of containers, screeching Buy Me! with their false claims and prices, miles of perjury. In the eerie lighting, the containers were brighter than the moist shoppers who hobbled between stereos, lubricants, lawn-furniture, Sleep-Ezes, greenest peas. Ten-thousand bright items and not one able to help me sail through that night. The merchandise came to a life more sacred than the shoppers, the sacrilege was touching. I stared too long at them, mumbling to myself, making some scurry away from me. Chattering, "Now that I'm free, why the fuck am I living like a clenched fist in that studio apartment I never want to go home to?"

She was buying fruit. Or testing it. Moving along the quartz-lit counters of color-enhanced produce. She'd pop a grape into her mouth or maybe a small radish. Who was she? So unlike the grey bundles shopping nearby. I watched her, fascinated. She was grazing like a deer.

What she was wearing was not important to me, but I noticed it anyway. A loose dress that I imagined she'd thrown over her nude body. Were those cream-colored stockings or was she cream-colored? Why was she wearing schoolgirl shoes with stocky heels? Her dark hair lay captured in a single wide clamp of engraved silver.

Dripping, in a raincoat that absorbed water instead of shedding it, I stood across the glowing fruit counter from her, staring in awe, fingering plums to avoid detection. She had a pretty, unblemished face, dark hair that would uncurl maybe to her shoulders. Fingers free of rings, except one. And maybe deep-ocean blue eyes. She seemed unconcerned about her beauty yet was beautiful and I sensed unavailable, in spite of her listless grazing at that late, late hour.

I probably didn't appear as depressed as I felt. I have a flat-back posture that never fails me and even in the deepest gloom I look rather alert. She did not; however, she looked stooped, on the brink of tears.

But isn't grazing shoplifting? Maybe I should present myself to her as Store Security and threaten to arrest her for felonious grazing, give her a brief speech on morals, suggest she join me for a cup of coffee, obtain her phone number, release her on parole. Why not? No, she'd probably laugh at me and reach for another blueberry. I couldn't approach her. Never. I couldn't risk the embarrassment of another outright rejection. I did not have a single drop of Italian blood coursing through my veins. I subdued my passion and quit stalking her. Maybe I was too depressed, too shy, and too comfortable within my pain. That is, too self-pitying, self-involved, and spoiled. Ah, well.

But we met. An amazing meeting, a writer's dream meeting, and at precisely the right moment in both of our lives. This is how it happened:

No longer stalking her, a derelict at sea again, by pure coincidence I drifted in behind her at the check-out counter, standing with my eyes half closed, trying to determine her perfume, if any. It turned out to be some marvelous French soap, she told me later. I continued to stand behind her, nearly touching her hair for the next five minutes, unable to speak. Then God winked at me. She picked up a copy of American Woman, opened to the index, and dropped it into her shopping basket, an issue that included one of my stories.

I followed her with my eyes. She walked to the automatic doors, realized it was still raining, turned and carried her bags to an adjoining coffee shop where she set them down in a booth and ordered coffee and pie.

She sat scanning the index again, then flipped the pages from back to front, stopping at my story, *An Eternity Past Midnight*, folded the page back, settled herself nicely in a corner of the booth, took a sip of coffee and began to read the words that I, without knowing it, had written to her.

I stood twenty feet behind her, examining the paint on the duct work overhead with grave concern. I let her read on. She turned the first page without looking up, barely finding her cup with her fingers. She turned the second page. She passed the part where Miranda's husband hangs himself with a noose made from her Bergdorf Goodman nightgown. She read on, past the part where Mark, Miranda's lover, is ironically blinded in her dead husband's wine cellar by an exploding bottle of his thousand-dollar champagne. She read for twenty minutes, without looking up except to receive an additional refill of coffee from the waitress.

I stood watching her. I let her read as far as the scene just before the ending, where Miranda's yacht, the Windsong, sinks, and the uneducated but stunning French seaman, Tristan, swims her to the safety of the volcanic island. At that moment, I chose to stop by her table.

Her lovely face was stripped of emotion, her eyelids were trembling. She glanced up and right through me without seeing me and turned back to the ending.

She read the last few paragraphs, clearly moved, sighed, closed the magazine as if it were a papyrus scroll, set it in front of her and smoothed it out. She sat there, drained, for a half-a-minute, still involved in the story, unable to move, then opened her purse and fished out a lone wizened cigarette from its bilge. I watched her light it with a gallant, willing-to-die-for-love gesture, staring out the plate glass window into the sodden night, watching the wet smears of light from the parking lot. All the while, she avoided looking at me. The flush of color came back into face. She relaxed. When she had displayed her wedding ring with a guard ring of small diamonds, she gaped at me with an are-you-still-here? look.

"What do you want?"

"May I sit down?" A pickup line on a rainy midnight in Seattle.

"Of course you can't," she whispered, still in the story, "Don't be ridiculous." She was beautiful.

I sat. I was as welcome as a well-publicized serial rapist. She reached for her purse.

"Don't go," I said. She would have to reach over me to get her two bags of groceries.

She signaled the waitress. We waited in silence for her to arrive. The waitress brought her the check.

"Would you call a security guard, please?" With one finger she slid the check toward her cup.

"I'll get the manager. The other guy's at lunch." The waitress eyed me with contempt and left us alone again.

"Funny they call it lunch," I said brightly, "even though it's past midnight."

She sat there, held in place by her grocery bags, looking away. Then to my delight, she re-opened the magazine and started reading the last page of my story again. I asked her if she was enjoying the story that, I couldn't help noticing, she was reading.

She speared me with a look. I was exactly who the story was not about. A pushy, horny, grungy male.

"*An Eternity Past Midnight*," I mused, "I was never crazy about that title," I added with a dry professional tone, "You?"

I could see it caught her off-guard. He knows the title, she was thinking. How?

Emboldened, I crossed my legs, smashing the table with my knee and spilling coffee on the beloved text. She whispered a curse and wiped it with her scarf.

"Sorry." I took a breath so that she wouldn't smell mine, leaned forward with a certain lunatic quality and whispered, "I am the author of that story."

"You are like hell," she said, bravely I thought, pretending to read again.

"Why don't you think I wrote it?"

"Because it was written by a woman and because only a woman could have written it." Still, without looking at me. "And Meg Highland is that woman." Obviously she did not consider herself in danger.

"I am Meg Highland," I said simply just as the waitress reappeared and stood at a reasonable distance like a referee.

"Is the manager coming?"

"Yes, miss. I found him in the rest room." The waitress left again to urge him on.

"Meg Highland's my pen name. I used to sail on a ketch called the Highland Light and I named her after that ketch."

How dangerous could I be?

"And my name's Joyce Carol Oates. I wrote *A Garden of Earthly Delights*," she said, displaying wit under fire. She was at her prettiest now; she'd heard all the pick-up lines, and there were probably so many harmless strangers like me, operating behind sickly masks, that it was amusing for her to sharpen her instruments. She wasn't angry or frightened, she started counting out change and laying it on the check.

"It's a very well-kept secret," I said, prolonging the delicious moments.

"It certainly is a very well-kept secret. Where's the manager? Don't you feel kind of ashamed?"

The manager appeared at the table, freshly rinsed, already embarrassed by his forthcoming duty. The waitress stood to one side, backing him up. He opened his mouth to speak. I selected that crucial moment to begin reciting the final lines of the story, looking directly at her across the table.

"Miranda was slipping away, drowning. She watched her bubbles rising above her toward the shimmering moon, wide on the sea's surface far overhead. Suddenly all sides were safe and she gave herself up to drowning, finally to being on the wrong side of life. Everything she'd loved had died, why not she? Now she was in the grip of the moon where she wanted to be. It was her time to die."

Her eyes never leaving me, the waitress sat down beside her without making a sound, listening. I continued from memory. My God, the waitress whispered.

"Suddenly Miranda felt an arm strong as ironwood gripping her waist, then another more gently, gently under her chin, guiding her to the surface. Tristan. He must have seen her jump from the deck of the Windsong, and try to swim ashore from the sinking yacht. His mouth was on hers, breathing life-giving air into her lungs. She felt new heat entering her loins. You must not die, he said in his primitive English, there is already not beauty enough in this world."

I paused, never for an instant taking my eyes from hers. She was glassy-eyed, as if she'd been clubbed.

The manager, listening to every word, cleared his throat, "Uh-m, miss ..." She shushed him with a wave of her hand.

"Go on," she said to me, with a curiously intense expression. I nodded.

"As the rim of morning calm rose above the calm volcano, across the calm sea, which now held the bones of the Windsong along with the bones of all her secrets, Tristan carried Miranda up the white sand toward the line of coconut palms.

"He laid her down on the soft grass. Tomorrow, I shall take you home, Mademoiselle.

"With her arm behind his neck, Miranda drew herself up close to his dark face. I am home, Tristan, was all she said before she lost herself within his grateful lips. The end."

She watched me bright-eyed, her mouth ajar, not knowing what to think, but starting to believe in the ridiculous.

The manager, a small man made of raw steak, wearing a bright apron, who wasn't getting it, looked from her to me and back to her. "What can I do for you, miss?"

"Nothing, thank you, you can go wash your hands if you haven't already." He turned, scorned but relieved, and left. The waitress, a fan, stood, watching.

"It's him," she said to the woman, "It's Mr. Highland."

"Do you still want me to go?" I asked with disgraceful humility.

"No, God no, of course not."

Relieved, the author of the Meg Highland stories settled back on luscious ground, ready to take thoughtful questions.

"If what you say is true..."

"And it is." I looked through the wet windows into the desolate street, giving her a chance to appraise my profile again. I continued to look like a wino, of course, but maybe now, a wino with a computer.

"She's my favorite writer. I've read every Meg Highland story there ever was." Her eyes welled with emotion, "I've written her fan letters."

"Did she answer you?"

"Well, Ms. Highland wrote me two very polite notes that explained why she was too busy to write me personally. I'm afraid they were identical. I understood."

I suddenly felt well-loved by someone fascinating.

She looked at me gravely. "How could you have written those beautiful stories?"

"I disliked the world; I disliked that I was alone in it; it was late and I couldn't sleep. Like tonight."

She seemed hurt. "You're lucky you can create beauty when you're angry." Her eyes really were deep-ocean blue.

"What do you do?"

She paused and smiled downward. "Cry, watch Brief Encounter again. Read Meg Highland." She smiled at me, remembering. "Call a friend."

"Who?" I paused, "D'you mind?"

"No, I don't mind at all. I call my ex-husband."

"You're not married?" I looked at her ring.

She shook her head, "I just wear this." She held her ring finger up.

"For sentiment?"

"For protection."

She said she'd exhausted the two girl-friends she'd clung to after the divorce.

She looked away at the waitress who was still in the neighborhood, studying our scene with open admiration.

"I love Meg's opinions, I use her optimism"

"Those are my opinions, my optimism."

"Oh, I've always wanted to write. One of my teachers said I had real talent. I wish I could."

I felt something the size of a crab lodging itself in my throat and try to turn around. "Would you like me to help you become a writer?" I didn't trust myself to breathe.

"I'd be honored. I'd do anything to learn."

I paused. I had dropped my seed into a moist furrow.

"We'll start tomorrow."

"Except that I'd want to be free of, you know..."

She paused nicely, reading my mind, and didn't say the word, entanglements. I couldn't blame her.

"Of course not," I said too loudly. "Professional. We'll meet at the Clarke Street library, teacher-student."

"I've just been through a master-slave arrangement and so I'm leery..."

I gave her all the time she needed to finish.

"Well, I was married to a celebrity, to be exact. Just let it go at that." She pushed a sigh across the table with the word celebrity.

When they'd met, her husband had been a mean, uncastable, small-part actor, a part-time salesman, his only interest had lain in fiddling with cars. Early in their marriage, he had gone on a audition and had abruptly been transformed into a personable game-show host. He had an easy way with people and a pleasant voice. But with change comes change. They'd moved to Los Angeles, changed their friends.

The only people she ever saw were those involved in his side-pocket of show business, self-centered people who were rude to her, and worried about things she didn't care about and who were only kind when it suited them to be. Her husband imme-diately became one of them.

"How will it end?" she asked.

"How will what end?" Our affair?

"*An Eternity Past Midnight.* It's a two-part serial."

"If you want, you can read the proofs they sent me."

Her face flushed. "That would be fantastic." There are so few compliments one can put to good use.

She hesitated. "Could you tell me just the last few sentences of the ending now? Please." I felt myself trying not to smile. Her please had turned this into foreplay.

"I adore your endings." I felt her examining my face for the first time.

This man looks safe and masculine, and there is something touching in his slight clumsiness. Horrible breath, too-long hair, unkempt, deep-set dark eyes, dark brow, good nose, unshaven, blemishes. Laugh-lines and thought-lines. He isn't that bad look-ing, just badly maintained. Maybe if I could get him to stop drinking ... Lincolnesque.

Kind of like the English associate professor she'd had at col-lege who'd become her counsellor, who'd politely asked her during her second counseling session if she would mind un-buttoning her cashmere sweater so that he might better admire her breasts, and who'd made love to her on the rug in his book-reeking office. It was a good memory. "Miranda doesn't die, does she?"

I smiled, shook my head, I hadn't lost a heroine yet, not in dozens of outings. "No," I said, "she lives."

"Tell me." She was a child with the covers pulled all the way up to her nose, begging for one more bedtime story.

The author of *An Eternity Past Midnight* brought an elbow up to the table, leaned forward on it and massaged his eyebrows.

He was thriving. This, what was happening to him, was improbable even for fiction. Recite his own words to this remarkable angel? He searched the ceiling, then began:

"They didn't touch. Tristan walked beside her into the moon-washed garden where they stopped and looked into each other's eyes, not thinking of anything but themselves and their impossible happiness. They only had tonight. The sea never knew what it had done.

"Tomorrow they will come for me," she said.

I stopped, lost. "Anyway, it goes something like that."

I shrugged.

"That's it?"

"Not quite." I'd gotten caught up in her intensely dependent look, making it hard for me to remember. I paused, looking from one deep-ocean blue eye to the other. Then the words came toddling home to me like sheep...

"Athens Airport, dawn. The morning after their final night. Miranda whispered, "Some things, you can't explain, Tristan, and if you try to, they go away." For a moment, everything else for them melted away into nothingness. Tristan was trying valiantly not to cry. They'd found the only thing worth finding in this weary, cynical world and now it was being taken away. She would serve two years in the penitentiary before they would touch again. From somewhere overhead a voice warned softly, "Last boarding for Flight 1 to New York,"

Tristan held her with his eyes. The two Greek guards from Interpol approached the couple tactfully.

"Please, Mademoiselle, it is the time," the taller guard said gently, his dark eyes glistening.

"How can I leave you, Tristan," she said. "Will you wait?"

He only nodded, "I shall be always here for you," Sadly, he let her hand her hand fall.

"I believe you." She turned away, and in a moment, without looking back, Miranda was gone. The End." I sighed.

She sighed, too. "That's beautiful."

"Yes, but possible?"

"Why not?"

"Well, look around you."

"But to have written that you must have felt ..."

Nothing, I had felt nothing. But I didn't say that. I said, "I was full of loneliness." Partly true, I was full of tequila. After all, the story's about some bimbo with dreams as big as her hair, who sleeps her way to the bottom.

But this perfect woman before me was a true romantic and I wasn't, and that was how it all started between us. She believed in what I considered to be impossible.

"How, I mean why, do you write under that name?"

"As I told you, the Highland Light is a ketch."

"Is there a Meg?"

"My mother."

"But why use a woman's name at all?"

I had never, in all my years of writing Meg Highland's stories, admitted to anyone, expect my publisher and a Basque cleaning lady, that I was really her. But something strange was happening to me that night.

"Women readers trust women writers. Also, the only story markets left are women's magazines, so by changing my male point-of-view to a female point-of-view, I turned my stories into women's stories." I didn't tell her the true reason I hid behind a dress: shame. I didn't tell her until later what I really thought of the Meg Highland books, nor that I was only able to write them under the influence of straight tequila.

Still, amid my bedazzlement, something struck me about her,

whoever she was, and that was this; she is no fool. Any woman who can mention Joyce Carol Oates and Meg Highland in the same sentence knows something I don't. If she likes my stories, there must be something more to them than I think I'm putting into them. Up until then, I thought my stories only attracted people I didn't want to know. And here was a revelation that would come back to haunt us later.

"Meg Highland's identity is our secret. If you tell anyone ... I couldn't take my eyes from hers and I didn't want to. "Now, will you please tell me your name?"

"You first." she said.

"I have a terrible name, I hate it, it's strange: Singer Sargent, sorry, but can you believe it? Ask my mother's family for a full explanation."

"My name's Stephanie. Like your Stephanie in This Night Must Never End. My mother calls me Stevie."

"Stevie. What do you want to call me? My mother called me Goaty."

"Why, Goaty?"

"Because I used to eat paper," I winced shyly. "It's true."

"I'm going to call you Goaty."

And that was a long time ago.

She was uncertain. She said she had been the youngest in a houseful of bigots and chauvinists. That this was still that way in her part of Oklahoma regardless of the progress with civil rights and feminism. That there were no drugs yet and everyone had a gun within a few feet of him. Her value lay in housework and babysitting and her future was pretty clear: marry and shut up. Even though the boys did and said what they wanted, she was expected to maintain her virginity and dodge the bear traps that lay in her path. She could barely speak above a whisper for fear of scathing criticism that was attached to anything she said or did. She began writing secretly about princesses who got what they wanted. Princes who listened. Every story had a happy ending even though the heroine never married but kept lovers.

She never wanted me to see these stories. She was embarrassed. She said they were amateurish. Childish. I told her I knew just the publisher. I had met a woman who asked me once if I ever had the bent to write a romance novel to please think of her first. What was her name, I had written it down somewhere, in a file I had labeled LAST DITCH SURVIVAL. There it was. I called. She had moved to another misty eyed publishing house and when I reached her it turned out that she was editor in chief and would be most receptive

One morning after we'd been married several months, I found a dozen neatly typed sentences lying on my desk:

She didn't ask how it was possible that the young lord's regiment had survived, she only knew that he was standing beside her and the atrium at Great House suddenly seemed flooded in golden sunshine.

She put her small hands firmly on her hips. "Now tell me again you love me, John," she commanded with mock seriousness.

He tried to obey, but Rosheen's lips were suddenly impetuously planted against his and instead of answering, he kissed her so deeply and so fully that it left her heart spinning. And all the while, Lady Balfour sat stiffly in the corner, pretending to sew the new tapestry.

And that's where they stopped. I was intrigued. Stevie was out shopping. When she came home I asked her if she knew anything about them. She blushed.

"I wrote them." I was amazed, I told her; I didn't know she could do that. Did I like it?

"Yes. Very much."

She flopped on the sofa. "Whew! I was terrified. I thought you'd hate it, Goaty."

"What happens next?"

"What happens next is...nothing."

We both laughed. I asked her why nothing else happened.

"Because it is the ending."

"Of what?"

"Of a Meg Highland book, Goaty."

"An entire book?"

"An entire book that you and I are going to write together."

Could we sustain a slim story for the entire length of a book? I had been barely able to sustain Meg Highland's world for eight thousand words, tops, without placing myself in a rehab clinic. I took what Stevie had written to my study and read it carefully again. I came back in an hour with some opening pages, trying to keep my language in her style. I sat her down and began reading it aloud:

The Viscount of Grantleigh yawned. He was bored. From the gallery he surveyed the candlelit party below him. The newly arrived guests from the Continent were writhing happily to a slow reggae. But the Viscount was hopelessly bored and here it was only Friday, with the forced activities of entire country weekend still lying ahead. He sensed Beech at his elbow.

"No more champagne, thank you, Beech."

"Your Lordship, a young Irish girl has entered Grantleigh without an invitation. We have requested that she leave at once but she insists on hearing it direct from 'Lord High Ass,' as she puts it."

"Oh?" He felt himself smiling.

"That's the one, down there, your Lordship, leaning against the arch. lookin' up at us with that smirk on 'er."

The young Viscount sucked in his breath sharply. She was a beauty, he thought, and would look a lot more beautiful galloping astride Piraeus, his great black stallion. She stared defiantly up at him from across the candlelit ballroom. Unruly, defiant, her pretty

Irish face was surrounded by black curls held in a gaudy red barrette, her eyebrows arched wildly above her dark eyes. Could they be blue? She wore a red dress, tautly bound in it, her lean but full body jolted to the music. By Heavens, was that a rip in her dress?

"More champagne, your Lordship?"

"I think, yes, Beech."

I stopped reading. Stevie shrieked with delight. "We can! I know we can!"

It grew and grew into *The Green Hills of Connemara*.

That first afternoon, we opened a bottle of good champagne and an iced bottle of Polish vodka and set out a few of our favorite pâtés and cheeses, caviars and smoked fish, and discussed the new book for as long as she was able to and I was conscious, until it grew light outside, and then we made love and fell into the sleep of other gods. When we woke, we settled on *The Green Hills of Connemarra* as the title and that afternoon we began writing it. A ritual was born.

We wrote it in five weeks, record time, equally, chapter by chapter, and signed it simply Meg Highland. We told each other we'd never had so much fun in our lives and I believed it. Lavender House in New York agreed to publish it in paperback. It sold 488,000-copies, nearly half-a-million.

For every one of our nine married years, Stevie and I followed this ritual when we built our books together, side by side, sometimes relieving ourselves of six Meg Highland books in one year, going through our writing ritual almost every two months as methodically as the tides rose and fell just beyond our Federal colonial home in Arcadia, Connecticut, just one good tennis ball bounce from the Sound.

The ritual seemed like good luck, so I insisted that we begin every book with Stevie's ending. Her ending provided us with a destination, a puzzle to me at first, but once solved, I'd set up the first chapter. She was the perpetual romantic optimist, and when we started writing each book, we'd set sail for her happy ending.

Together we became one Meg Highland, and Meg Highland became a much more famous author than she'd ever contemplated as a magazine-story writer. And richer. Her lavender covered paperback books were seen in rows lining every supermarket library; she had grown from having a cult following into a being a form of soft-dietary nourishment that a million disorientated American women could not live without.

Ours was that rarest of all marriages, a true trade union. We wrote together interchangeably, sitting at opposite tables. We were co-workers, friends, lovers.

An ideal bond bound us together, and the few friends who shared our secret, agreed. Even when we squabbled about our characters and storylines, it was fun. Fun because I didn't give a damn about the outcome; it was always fine. Our output stood at thirty-six Meg Highlanders. It was a perfect marriage.

Of course, there were times when my wheels would stop turning. Caught between chaise longue and balcony in our candlelit, dark-velvet-and-silver-wine-goblet hell, writing about driven men and cornered women clinging to each other against an unjust world. Always with the same interlocked fingers and souls, blinded by their self-absorption, and at the end, squinting into a new valley, as the egg-yellow sun slid behind the lilac-green tinted hills; sustained only by their love and their naive hopes for a forever of pure bliss. The triumph of narcissism over an uncaring society.

We'd become a two-headed book-writing gorgon. It wasn't enough to have written these thirty-six books; I now realized I had long ago begun to justify them. If I had been embarrassed when I'd met Stevie, I was now in full denial. And though I joked about them while we were writing them, on the great morning after, I felt entombed inside them because I now knew

I'd been ridiculing myself.

Everyone looks happy. Look at these photographs again. Our excellent tennis court with its dreadful tennis, our tension-filled catered soirees with their extravagance of faux celebrities out from the city; a dignified lady who destroys people in the media; a bug-like news man who celebrates monsters; a television lawyer who advertises perjury, highly-placed money handlers, laughing bankers, top executive sycophants, lawyers able to represent either side.

If you're hungry, just ring the kitchen. It was all loud and empty, and more frequently, humiliating, the forced give-and-take that a complacent society demands. Look at the mansions. The fullness of their views is in direct proportion to the emptiness of the viewers.

The ingenious torment of my past: All I had wanted to do was to write, the great luxury; to earn a living speaking from my soul, the evacuation of my soul. No one here gets it about being rich and not having money. They all have dreams as fat as their Republican asses. And I was among them.

I didn't realize how much I was drinking again. More and more I felt lost. But how can you be lost if you don't know where you're supposed to be?

Stevie saw it, of course; she wasn't blind, but she believed in our stories. She truly believed in the love they stood for. And she continued to write her proposed endings and leave them on my desk:

Jason found her mouth and, with his lips against hers, held her prisoner. She did as his mouth demanded. He'd carried her through Hell and out the other side...why not toward Heaven? Now, with Jason's bare arms around her waist there was no more fear, no more worry, and they had time, just a little more time, to fulfill every single one the joys they wanted. THE END. (Eventually from *The Southern Cross.*)

But sometimes, as with this ending, I was unable at first to respond with a beginning. So, after a few days, another ending appeared:

A sun-brightened smile curved Natascha's lips. It caught a tear as it rose in her eye and ran down her cheek, "Will you be leaving Leningrad tomorrow?"

Marc smiled the lopsided grin that had always made her heart race and he lifted her high in my arms.

"Not without you, my darling." He was a weary traveler who'd come at last to the end of his journey.

And with her yellow hair trailing over his bare shoulders, he carried her through the gallery, across the great marble hall and up, up the wide staircase. While outside the sun glistened on quiet white drifts of newly fallen snow. THE END. (From A Russian Spring.)

Stevie was unwilling to confront the central problem; that I needed rehabilitation time away. Away from my drinking, away from Arcadia, and especially away from Meg Highland, so that I could maybe begin to think about working on my epic novel, *The Sea Is Not Full,* that I had begun writing years before, a novel that spanned from the early 1800s to the present time, about a Jewish family, the Samuels, that survives both World Wars, travels half the world, and finally settles in Israel. A novel that I could sign with my true name. But after nine years of Meg Highland, I had begun to wonder if I could still write anything that asked a question more difficult than Would Derek come back to Helene? I'd made Stevie's dream come true, alright; I'd obeyed her fantasy to the letter and, most important, given her an outlet for her deepest feelings of love, brought her up to a fair standard of writing. When we'd first been married, she'd been overwhelmed by the idea of actually making a living saying what she felt about love. And there her fantasy stopped.

I was and will always be fifteen years older than Stevie, and when we met I had already written dozens of Meg Highland stories, all of which she'd read. As far as she was concerned, she believed that the unimaginable had happened; she had learned how to write books that were read by millions of readers, and I had taught her how. One night she woke me excitedly and told me that she now had the four impossible luxuries any woman could ever hope for in life. She had found a man she deeply loved. She had something fulfilling to do every day. She always had something to look forward to. She always had something to dream for.

She'd married me out of love, she said, but she'd also gotten herself a mentor, a writing partner, and a best friend, a man she could fully trust. She'd gotten that.

And of course I'd found love, but the best thing I could say about our marriage was that it was friendly and safe. Fulfilling creatively? No.

In our books, I thought I'd crossed the line of pleasant repetition to deadly repetitiousness. You can't compromise too long. When I'd first decided to hide behind a woman's name and invented a tall woman named Meg Highland, I'd meant for her to live for maybe two or three years then die violently, until I could get enough money to live on so that I could finish writing *The Sea is Not Full.*

Now we had all the money we needed. Had I given too much of myself away, writing about the power of a love I didn't believe in?

That was when I decided we should have our late honeymoon. It was to be a damage-control inspection honeymoon to see if I still had something I was able to write about. To see if we could still locate each other, to find out if our writing had disguised us both and turned our marriage into one of Meg Highland's costume balls. Her name was never to be mentioned during our time in Europe.

But before we could leave, we had contracted to deliver one

last book to Lavender House to fulfill our annual quota.

And one morning on my desk, I found Stevie's ending to the book that was destined to destroy Meg Highland:

Suddenly Clarissa knew that this was the beauty the Marquis had promised to carry them both to, to the heart of the sun. "Take me there, my darling," Clarissa whispered. "Now," her lips against his. She felt his bare chest pounding against her breasts and suddenly she realized there was absolutely nothing for her to fear, nothing left for her to say. THE END.

In an hour I had finished chapter one:

"General Hood paced before the tall Palladian windows, watching his red-coated troops parade on the vast lawns of the castle. The roomful of officers studied him, waiting for his command. At last, the general spoke.

"Napoleon has flanked us and by God there is only man in England who can get our message through to him."

Gasps.

"Send for that young Marquis, will you? I can't stomach the boy, personally, cheeky rascal, but he's the only one in the regiment who speaks fluent French as well as Mandarin. And," the General added sourly, "plays a damned decent chucker of polo."

"You don't mean Alexander, the Marquis of Fallbridge, do you sir?" The name alone made the General wince.

"Him. He's the one, wretched scoundrel."

"But, General, the Duke has never forgiven him for his behavior at the hunting lodge with young Lady Spence..."

"And never will I daresay. The Duke must not learn of our masquerade. The Marquis will ride in disguise." He scanned the huge library, catching the eyes of two field generals, a commander, a prince, and his own daughter, Clarissa. "You must all swear to silence."

They nodded their assents.

"But no one knows where the devil he is, General."

The sergeant-at-arms standing at attention near the door saluted. "Will you grant me permission to speak, General?" The general nodded. "They say he's borrowed your sloop and sailed it to Paris for the Bal des Amateurs."

"Damned fop," cursed the general.

"Typical," sighed the prince.

The others gave each other perplexed glances. An uneasy silence filled the Great Hall.

Clarissa, the general's daughter, abruptly broke the silence. "He's not in Paris, Daddy, " she said in her small voice.

The general wheeled and confronted his only daughter.

"Then where, child?"

"Alex," she began, then turned her wide-set eyes skyward, indicating the chambers of the west wing where she had spent her childhood and adolescence. She smiled sweetly and uttered two words with pride, "Asleep in my nursery, Father."

As one man, the room gasped at this fearless confession to such a deed of impropriety. Bed General Hood's virgin daughter? Someone gasped, "Knave." A junior officer muttered, "Rascal." A dragoon unsheathed his sword, "Swine."

The General recoiled. The picture alone of a king's dragoon asleep amid dolls made him flush with rage.

Controlling his famous temper, the general smiled at his daughter. "Well, my dear, if you can spare him for his King, run upstairs and fetch him."

Presently Alexander the Marquis of Fallbridge, all of twenty-two, joined the men in the Great Room. His boots and uniform were neat but his long pale hair was wild. As he passed into the room he took a metal goblet and held it before a butler who filled it with wine. General Hood explained the dangerous mission. He would need to dress as a woman. The young dragoon smiled and raised his goblet.

"For God for country and for Clarissa!" he drank it dry and held it toward the footman who replenished it.

"What about King George?"

"I am not speaking with his majesty until he apologizes for fondling Clarissa's —"

"Right." General Hood was clearly taken aback. He was facing the only man who could save the empire.

"Right you are, Alexander," the general chuckled at the daring lieutenant, "Then let's get on with this bloody war, what?" The men laughed, the crisis had passed.

To fulfill our Lavender House book contract, we'd begun to write our thirty-seventh Meg Highlander. And the corrosion that had been creeping into our marriage came out as rust in a series of small arguments. The first was over the book's title, *In the Service of the King,* (mine) or *The Wine of Love,* (Stevie's).

It was laughable that I even cared enough to argue about a title, but I did. After all these years, I knew we would never graduate to writing anything remotely true to life, so what difference could the title make?

Suddenly Meg Highland was no longer possible. And for the first time, her spotless career had been indelibly stained. I was through with her. Our late-autumn book was never delivered to Lavender House; whatever its title, it was left unwritten. We closed the house indefinitely, left Arcadia behind, and flew to Sweden to pickup our new car and begin our long postponed honeymoon, leaving Meg Highland behind us forever.

I caught up with Stevie on the steps of the Berne Clinique des Femmes, startling her out of a daze. She really hadn't seen me. I took her arm and we continued down the steps into the shockingly brilliant afternoon. I could feel her arm trembling through her coat and I knew better than to ask until we could sit down someplace. I think I was frightened.

It was tea time.

"Let's have cream tea at the Palais Hotel," I guided her elbow. Cream tea at the Palais was one of our unchecked-off must-do things on our check list. An English custom. She didn't answer.

"Oh, come on, Mrs Sargent, it's jam cakes and we're consenting adults."

"Oh, Goaty." I could barely hear her.

On the way to the hotel she took my hand and held it with the grip of a day-old baby. She stared straight ahead. The lucid winter air was making our eyes water, but it did not brace us, not today, it merely entered us and left us brittle, wanting to be indoors.

It wasn't until we'd been seated by a sunny window among palms, far from the violins and tea dancers, could she tell me that her brain scans had shown an inoperable tumor. I felt the air rush out of me; I felt my head tip toward the floor. I asked her to dance, as calmly as I was able to. The instant we stood up, I still see as if it were a painting. The sun glaring down on the long stone courtyard, the skylight high overhead, formal waiters standing still, two couples on the floor, laughing and chatting, moving naturally to the music, *Vous, Qui Passe Sans Me Voir,* a delicate French song of inexorable frustration about a woman who never sees the man who loves her. It was all too bright.

Dancing, I kissed Stevie and told her we'd get another opinion, that we had plenty of time to be sure, that there were experts here in Switzerland. I said something I'd remembered from our marriage vows. She told me that the symptoms would be painless and quick. It might happen anytime, possibly while she slept. She said without emotion that she'd always been expecting something like this, because our life together had been too perfect. That I should forget about our silly squabbles, that nothing she'd ever said about our differences meant anything, that I had simply spoiled her, and that was all; she was grateful for everything. She told me not to be sad, that she had been given nearly ten ideal years, more than any woman could hope for. She said that when we'd fallen in love in Seattle, I had taken her off the ledge of suicide, and that when we'd married, all she had ever prayed for were these ten years of happiness, and she had been given that. What more could she ask? She had been granted her wish. We were unable to stop dancing and trying to cry invisibly. The violinist, wearing a black tie and dinner jacket, caught my eye, nodded respectfully and winked. Respectfully, like Death.

Later, in bed, unable to sleep, discussing what we should do, she decided that we wouldn't rely on medical genius, that we'd have no indignities. We would go off by ourselves, somewhere, and live "our last wave by" together. Lying side by side in the thick darkness, touching along our lengths, it made her cry to hear me cry.

In the morning, Stevie suddenly hated the Swiss. For no rational reason that she could think of, the Swiss suddenly appalled her. With their little Swiss Army knife tweezers and their dull, clean cooking and their choppy Germanic language and their unnaturally neat streets. How dare they be smug? Berne was an ugly city by any standard, and the Swiss could scrub their sidewalks until they bled, but everyone knew that below them lay vaults filled with stacks of gold bullion, the pilferings of the world's richest shysters. Bank accounts full of stolen money. The Swiss were filthy. She had to get away immediately.

"Please, Goaty, can we leave?"

Later, in Venice, when she could laugh about it, she told me that she simply didn't want to be caught dead in Switzerland.

We crossed the border into France just before midnight near Chamonix, and over the next few weeks we drove south, staggering back and forth across the map, east and west, looking for somewhere to settle, stopping at farm inns, visiting medieval ruins.

We drove to Lyon to get away from our routine of inns and ruins, and fell into the enforced revelry of its discotheques, tried night-long parties with strangers, but it was only a sour obligation.

Stevie didn't need to say goodbye to anyone in Arcadia, just mail couple of pretty cards saying that she probably wouldn't be coming back. I never read the letter she wrote to her mother. Lavender House didn't need to know. And there had been no children in our lives. I hadn't wanted children at first and she'd agreed with me, then when we changed our minds and wanted children, it never seemed to be the right year.

Always now when I woke in the middle of the night, I reached for her, was she alive? I listened for her breath; I touched her to feel her warmth. One night in a village called Cogolin, she wasn't in bed when I reached out to touch her. I sat up, startled, then saw her outlined against the window sitting in a chair. The tranquilizer had worn off. The street lamp made her a halo, because our room was on the premiere etage. Someone up the street was playing a flute near an open window.

Our inability to make a decision about where to live was tiring, the doubt was exhausting her.

"How's your head?" My voice startled her. The familiar question.

"No pain, darling," she said lightly.

Our words hung in the room between us and the mad flowery wallpaper on the ceiling, and the dark opening in the armoire that wouldn't close. Then we both started to speak at the same time and we both stopped. I waited for her to begin again.

"Oh, Goat, I'm afraid I don't know how to die."

"Who's an expert at that?" I said, fully awake now. "Once we get away from the medical geniuses, we're on our own, aren't we?" I always said we, as if I could include myself in her dying, but I couldn't help feeling I was patronizing her death. She never mentioned it.

"Goat, do you think I'm being punished for something?"

I took a while to answer. "Probably." I tried to keep it light. "God's punishing you for writing thirty-six dishonest books about love."

She didn't laugh. She'd moved herself entirely into each book, fully devoted to each one of our characters.

"I believed every word I wrote."

"I know you did."

"We wrote them together."

But I'd written them from some secondary force I'd found living inside me, and she knew it.

"So, He's punishing me, too," I said.

"You're not being punished."

"Oh, yes I am." I said it too quickly.

"Do you still love me?"

"I still love the way you change the subject, and I'm also doubling your tranquilizer prescription."

She clung to me, her naked arms circling my chest. "Will you have me?" she whispered.

"Yes, of course I'll have you," Harry sighed lovingly, tears streaming down his cheeks. He stretched his arms toward the welcoming moon and shouted, "Forever!" THE END. (From To a New Land" by Meg Highland.)

Of course her dying was up to her. The manner of it, of course, not the timing. And we did talk.

One morning after breakfast at a farmhouse inn, driving along a shaded country road, she said:

"Thank God the earth is round, I can't imagine a life without sunsets and sunrises."

"Here's to God," I added.

"Sometimes I think our conversation can save our world."

"Not this conversation."

"No, but some of them. We talk, Goaty. We talk about everything. Other people don't talk."

"I thought other people talked too much," I said.

"It's just big words, crammed into small minds, they repeat stuff they've heard, it's data. I mean we talk, the way people used to."

"Maybe you're right." Conversation was keeping her windows open to a better view.

And when we talked, it was about love and death and fear. Sometimes, usually in the dark, when Stevie was without the protection of light, she made me tell her about the things we were never going to be able to do together and I would tell her the things we'd done together. She would ask me what I would do with myself after she died, if I would continue being Meg Highland. No, I told her, I would make Meg Highland comfortable under a guillotine. Would I marry again? No, not marry. Please, I want you to. But I don't want to marry again, I would tell her, only because I truly couldn't imagine it.

We talked about the anger everywhere in the world that we could do nothing about, and we felt the helplessness that dying people have always felt, leaving the world worse than when they came to it. She told me about her dreams. That she'd been dreaming of our house in Arcadia and our children who were always eating. But of course, we had no children and never did.

She was facing her dying far better than I was facing her dying. One night, I told her that sometimes I felt the guilt of an innocent bystander.

She said, guilt? She told me that she'd always carried an invisible bundle of guilt; that she never deserved to be happy because she never felt worthy of our life, and so had always been expecting her accounts someday to be balanced, and now they were. All her life she'd glimpsed death whenever she'd been extremely happy. I told her I'd never known any of that garbage.

So on we drove. We passed through Tuscany without seeing it but slept in its villages for a week. We were losing our life together and not doing it right.

As we drove back out of Italy and as far east as Trieste, her dying became an epic natural force. I watched it naturally growing inside me and I saw its truth again and again in the faces of the people who knew and in the streets and churches of each new village. Wherever I drove, there it was.

Often, anytime, now she'd talk about the quality of our love. "What grade would you give us? Tristan and Isolde? Heloise and Abelard?" she'd ask.

Their eyes met for an instant. All they could see was the fire of their love leaping wildly between them, a leopard flame.

"Forever," Jonathan vowed simply, "and beyond forever."

"For-ever and beyond forever," Susan repeated against his lips, her cheeks wet with tears. Suddenly Jonathan swept her up in my arms, lifting her high, and all the world was lit in golden sunlight. "We've won, my darling, the world belongs to us!" And it was true. The world had been theirs for the asking, and they had asked. THE END. (From *A Fool's Carnival* by Meg Highland.)

Then to Venice. It was suddenly winter, the dark tide rose above the stone embankments, and we found a Pensione near

Salute that was nearly empty, owned by Signora Margherita, a woman whose face over the years had been built by sorrow upon sorrow. At first we slept at odd hours and ate ripe berries and cantaloups without appetite.

But a strange thing happened between us in Venice.

In Venice we made love as we never had before, furiously discovering each other's limits for the first time in our lives. Stevie asked me to punish her, to bind her, to slap her buttocks. Why?, I asked. Because I'm leaving you. Risking each other, feverishly hurting each other with a vivacious sexual anger. The safest anger we'd ever known. As if to blame the other for the death of our snug, smug life. And after making love, we'd collapse into a blackness without memory, that in its void resembled the atheist sleep of a perfect death.

Every time we came in or went out, Signora Margherita would crank her pullet neck at an angle as we passed her table to regard us with a dark look of awed approval. Sometimes we heard her sigh. Her face cleared of sorrow, she would croon Buon giorno, and so would we. Our operatic lovemaking had apparently touched a chord.

Never saying anything to Stevie, I constantly watched for her symptoms.

"It's important to die in Venice," she said one day, as if to die in Venice was something of a coup, a tradition to conform to.

"Because of that book?"

"No, but it's an old city of ghosts and Death is just another guest invited to the Carnevale."

Sometimes now in the daytime Stevie sat and cried, once all afternoon alone in the worn-down Cathedral of the Redentore. She was overwhelmed by what was coming to her but she felt it was an old thing, too, and familiar. In that grandiose, sculptured city, she felt that she was joining the thousands of hands that had created the Venice she saw, standing comfortably around her.

One morning Signora Margharita came to us sadly to say that the Quaresima Carnevale was beginning Thursday and that her Pensione had been fully reserved. Would it disturb us to surrender our room? Of course not. We had never told her how long we intended to stay. She was molto desolato. Please come back. I will miss you. Love such as yours...she gasped, spread her hands and looked toward heaven and smiled angelically. It was a fine time to leave Venice; there was a bite in the air. And Stevie's not dying there had freed us for the remainder of our lives together, however brief.

Much later, I found out that she had let herself get pregnant in Venice. She was never able to tell me.

"I've been thinking," she began.

I touched her hair to let her know that I was conscious. I couldn't remember where we were.

"I've been thinking, can we write a book?"

"Screw Meg Highland," I said into my pillow. I drifted to sleep for an instant then snapped awake. "No, let's do it, let's write a horror book, The Slow but Painful Death of Meg Highland."

"Not about her, Goaty, about us, about our life together, and what's happening to me. I think it would be interesting.

"Interesting?"

"I think you could make it fine."

"Really? Do you think we should start something new?"

"Meaning: Do I have the time left?"

"No, just why don't we take it easy?"

But still in my sleep, I felt a surge run through me, the first surge that had once forced me to know I had to become a writer. A cool rush up from my stomach. I was afraid I couldn't write a book, not about us, flesh-bound lovers. But I didn't say that.

"What's our title?"

"I don't know."

In Mestre, not far from Venice, the next day we bought an Olivetti portable typewriter and a large, hardcover notebook. Whoever wasn't driving would write down events and we'd date them in their order, remembering as best we could, anecdotes, thoughts, or whatever the other was saying at the moment. And each night wherever we were we'd type our notes from the notebook, taking turns at the typewriter.

After another week in the low Tuscan hills we decided to go back over the border into France, and only on instinct stopped at a six-room hotel in a village twenty miles inland from the Mediterranean set among the national forest in the mountains of Le Var.

The village was silent except for the tink-tink of the bell ringing from its ancient church, and we were drawn to the cafe in the mornings where we each had our bowl of café-au-lait, bread and butter. A few workmen on their way to work, wearing clean shirts and overalls, stopped for their cafés and cigarettes inside, playing the pinball machine, ping-ping-bong-bong. But outside at the wood table we usually sat alone. I had noticed the owner, a woman, watching us each morning through the glass for nearly a week. I had gotten used to the French staring at us. We'd been warned about the chill of the Parisian, not the French.

"Pardonnez moi, madame, monsieur. Permettez moi?" She sat down with grave respect and smiled. The woman introduced herself, Madame Lejeune, and told us she'd been watching us and she thought that something might be terribly wrong with madame, was she mistaken? After a moment of surprise, Stevie shrugged and said, Non, Madame, vous n'avez pas trompe. I looked away while Stevie told her. Madame Lejeune was deeply grieved but she said she had known it. How? One knows these things.

It would be possible, if we would please pardon her presumption, for us to stay at the hameau that her brother looked after. He was the caretaker and alone there. It was a matter of six little kilometers from her café, not more.

Madame Lejeune's generous, well-furnished face, was filled with dramatic angles, perfectly-suited for either warmth or anger, joy or grief. Her offering to Stevie, and to me, had been given from pure kindness. Impossible. No money would change hands, Madame Lejeune emphasized firmly. Non! She held her hand up and repeated rapidly, Non-non-non, only pay for the croute (the crust, or food), and the bois de chauffage for our fireplaces.

An hameau, it turned out, is a hamlet, usually a group of stone houses built by one extended family or several, not far from one another, in a remote area, too small to be called a village, without church or mayor, but with a well and a central stone barn.

This hameau had been built in the early 1800s and abandoned before the turn of the century. There were a dozen small stone houses, some connected, and a main house that had once been the barn. It was beautiful in a rugged way, built in a rugged canyon, set among bristling hills in a hostile country of steep slopes. Two families had once hunted there and raised goats and chickens and grown olives, chestnuts, grapes, lavender. It had been bought and resuscitated twenty years before by a wealthy English family who came there to stay each summer for a month. They'd kept its ancient name, "Le Nid du Renard." The Nest of the Fox. Stevie and I were overwhelmed by the Madame Lejeune's kindness.

It was truly abandoned. I drove the final two kilometers over a frame-cracking cleared roadway that gave way to natural outcroppings of the hills' living rock faces.

It always transformed any trip we made to the outside world into an expedition. In the village there were only Renault camions and small trucks and we rented one of those.

When we met him, Madame Lejeunes' brother, Bob (Baub), seemed distant to us; I believe without meaning to be. He'd lived alone as caretaker for so many years that he'd gotten more used to being with wordless beings, dogs and goats and roosters and himself, than with outsiders. If he seemed remote to us, it was a normal country remoteness. Le Nid's houses had all been built rough-hewn, of grey stone with slate roofs. Bob occupied the house that had originally been the barn. We chose a two-story house down the hill. We had electricity, a fireplace upstairs and one down, and a working bathroom. Seven pieces of simple furniture from the last century, including an armoire, stood in our bedroom and loomed cotton mats warmed areas of the stone floor. Two framed engravings of dour-looking birds hung above the bed. A small collection of primitive paintings of ships and goats surrounded the main fireplace downstairs, down the curving stone staircase to the front door. All the windows were deep-set through two-foot thick plastered walls, whitewashed in all the rooms. She knew at first glance this would be an adequate house for her to die in. Far better than any hospital. At last, she was chez elle.

Our first afternoon there, we gathered a hundred fallen chestnuts under the loaded trees on a level glade, up a nearby hill. That night we slit them, roasted them in the fireplace in a long-handled pan with holes in the bottom, and made our dinner from the blackened chestnuts, with wine, bread, Camembert and Roquefort cheeses from the village.

In all our time there, we rarely saw Bob, only sometimes aware of him up the hill, planting or repairing.

He rode his bicycle to the village once or twice a week and apparently knew nobody well enough to have them visit him.

The wintry days weren't long now. They began to grow dark before four o'clock each afternoon, they aged badly, beginning after lunch when the day abruptly became old.

Lying in bed in the early morning Stevie would count measures between the gallant battle cries the of the rooster, Coco, trying to count herself back to sleep. When she had nearly faded back into drowsiness, the goat we had befriended, Mickey, would butt on the door downstairs with his horns.

"Goaty, tell me, did you really used to eat paper? Was it like Mickey? Or would you just nibble it?"

"Like Mickey."

"But would you swallow it?"

"Never on the first date, darling."

"We've got a book to finish, Goat boy; get your ass out of bed," she'd usually say something in that vein, and we'd get up.

We would stop writing at midday. We'd eat lightly, a cold langoustine, or jambon and cheese and, of course, bread, and always one of the tough local wines; then we'd lie down. Stevie had noticed amber seepage maps here and there on the walls and we would stare at them during our afternoon nap and imagine human and animal shapes and discuss their sex lives. Later, I'd bring her coffee and we'd sit outside in the chill air, looking toward the cleft in the hills where the sun would set. The black, serious coffee, the almost-sour local milk, heated, and sugar cubes that looked as though they'd been quarried. We drank tea in Switzerland and Connecticut but could never imagine drinking in Italy or France. It was a ritual we both relied on; though like our other rituals, it never fooled the clock.

One night after we'd divided three bottles of crude Provençal rosé and fallen into bed, leaving our scraps of food on the table downstairs, Stevie woke to hear tiny chattering coming from downstairs.

"Mice!" she whispered, and woke me.

"Probably only rats." We listened.

"I knew it!" she said, "I always suspected rats were French. Listen, it's unmistakable, they're speaking French."

I listened and they were. "But with a Parisian accent," I noted. We never again left our scraps of food on the table, nor did we divide three bottles of rosé.

Stevie titled our book "All That Matters," and it came quickly. As it went, beginning at Berne and going backwards down through our life in Arcadia all the way back to our first moment at the supermarket in Seattle, it would end here, at Le Nid, a chronicle of the years of our lives lived together, through my last day alone, simply told.

Was it painful for her to speak about the truth, her death, for me to write about our lives in the past tense?

Yes. But writing it together kept her mind excited, and of course, it meant more to me than any book I'd ever written. But no book, no matter how fine, could reclaim our life together.

I didn't know if I would even be able to write the last few pages by myself. Why? To keep some drowsy matron awake at the beach? In keeping with our outline, obviously I would be alone writing them. Would I write them at Le Nid du Renard? How would she die? Would the instant come without warning? Would we be sitting outdoors, and suddenly she'd spill coffee, dropping her cup and saucer on the frozen ground?

Stevie was exhausted from watching for symptoms, waiting for them to show. Though she had been told she was dying and had actually studied her MRI brain scan and understood what the thing was that was going to kill her, she was bored by the tension of waiting every minute for fatal symptoms. As for me, if ever I went anywhere alone, as always, I would hurry back more quickly than I'd gone out, never certain that I would find her living.

"Take me home," she whispered against his lips, as she gave herself to his mouth. She was his and he was hers, completely, and she knew whatever lay ahead, their love was eternal. She had found the answer at last. It was Jeremy. THE END. (From This Night Must Never End by Meg Highland.)

All That Matters was finished. Except for my last few pages, of course, it was ready to be shipped to our publisher.

I left Stevie sitting by the fire with a pyramid of chestnuts beside her, a knife in her hand, and the large skillet that had small flame holes cut in the bottom.

I took a walk. The afternoon was chill and the terrain surrounding Le Nid turned any walk into a hike. There'd been goat and cow trails made in the 1800s grown over now and these were where I walked. It was ugly country, there were no great bursts of green, thorny with sudden outcroppings of rock. But I walked out, away from the house under the pale, dead sky.

What I'd always enjoyed about a setback, when I'd been able to grab one by the neck, was that it brought out the strength hiding in me, the rational, the calm. Finding good lying around in myself had always been great validation.

But what was happening wasn't a setback, and even if it were, it had me by the neck. I didn't even care if I never saw the best in myself again. I detested my writing, and what little I'd done with it. I detested my good health. I wanted my own brain tumor.

I was down by the spring now, shrouded away from the sky by an arbor of oak trees that never lost its leaves.

The ground spring had been walled up in the early 1800s and beside it a laundry basin the size of a sarcophagus had been cut into to the living rock. I stood a long time by the chilled pool.

No tears at our funerals, please. Appear stalwart. Throwing

oneself into the grave of one's lover is awkward, beyond outré. A dozen sessions of grief counseling with a calming therapist will put it all behind you. Get on with the business of living. Sans regrette.

I could not imagine ever putting it all behind me. To redirect my dead love into a fresh love for someone else; I could not imagine even caring about another woman. Some men are monogamous and I realized I was among them.

I smiled as I thought: You see it in elephants and mynah birds. Dogs. When a man has been close to the one woman who can translate the world for him into a fabulous odyssey, why would he want to try the trip again on a bus ticket?

The water was dark and undisturbed. I stood a long time, knowing the truth. Then I realized, I would rather die beside Stevie than be alone. Maybe here would be the place.

Something splashed. A snail had dropped from an overhanging walnut branch into the chilled water. I reached out and in my curled hand brought the barely floating snail back into the air and set it on the tree trunk, holding it in place until it was warm enough to cling for itself. I've written poems to hawks and blossoms of fire, never to a snail.

There was logic to my decision that a snail should be allowed to live, not die. Or that I might kill and eat a bird. But there was no logic here; I was surprised at the anger I felt over Stevie's dying and I traced it to unnatural selection. The Doktor at Treblinka decided which inmates should die and which should live, and there is even logic in monsters. I had selected myself.

Tears blinded Lara's green eyes. "Do we dare risk the rest of our lives together?" she wept. Her tears shone in the moonlight. "We have so little time."

Ian smiled the uneven smile that she'd first fallen in love with.

"You little fool, don't you see, our love is all that matters." is

hands were hot ingots against her bare waist. She tried to speak, but he silenced her mouth with his and carried her across the beach to the boat waiting in the white sand to take them back to their secret island where they would be alone with each for all the days and nights remaining to them. THE END. (From *Lara's Moon* by Meg Highland.)

I cut some sprigs of lavender to lay on our bed for Stevie to discover before she went to sleep that night. I hiked back in the thickening light, well before nightfall.

By the time I opened the door to our stone house, I had decided how to do it. The next morning I would drive to Toulon and buy enough Amphodons to put down a pair of rhinos.

It was late afternoon of the following day by the time I had driven back from Toulon through a cold windy rain. Stevie had been keeping both fireplaces alive, and we had glasses of thick, warm red wine with our clabbered cheeses on petit pains. Earlier in the day, I had sealed the manuscript pages of *All That Matters* in a box and addressed it to our publisher in New York. I had written letters of explanation to various people, Stevie's mother, Bob, Madame Lejeune, the publisher, which would be read afterward.

We sat downstairs. We weren't talking for a few minutes, listening to music on the radio, to the rain and to the fire, when I thought I heard the sound of a car. From the window, I could see one crawling toward our house, down the steep road. It was grey with road powder, streaked from rain; a road-weary Alpha Romeo sedan, it turned out to be. Since we'd lived there, no one except us had ever driven in to Le Nid du Renard.

The man who got out of the Alpha was not tall and wore his fedora pulled down. He stood in the drizzling rain and stretched his back and legs and looked around for a moment, then seeing smoke from our chimney, walked toward our house with a quick limp, maybe stiff-legged from driving a good distance. I told

Stevie about our visitor and we watched him from the window until he disappeared under the wet overhanging green between the houses.

Stevie went back to the fire and waited. We heard tapping and I saw his face at the window. He seemed to be grimacing. I went to the door. When he entered and shook his wet hat Stevie recognized him right away. Doctor Pontebianco.

"Do you remember me, Signora?" he was a short, strong man, nearly bald, with a rich moustache and oversized teeth. Stevie had named him Dr. Bullet.

"Dottore Pontebianco." She said in perfect Italian.

I saw the doctor's eyes were wet at the edges and I felt a cool cramp grip my stomach. Why had Pontebianco come all this way?

"This is my husband, Dottore, Mr. Sargent." She sat quickly by the fire. The men shook hands.

"You drove all this way?" I asked with stupid heartiness. What more could I do? Feeling pale and far too tall, I stood by the fire and gripped the slate mantel. Pontebianco, a man we hardly knew, had driven 400 kilometers to see us.

"You have no telephone." The doctor smiled for the first time, "I like this country. Myself, am from Torino."

"How on earth did you find us?"

"I see the name of this village on your postmark and I simply drive, drive, drive. Madame Lejeune at the cafe, kindly tell me. I am so relieved to find you, Signora Sargent. I have news. I have excellent news for you."

"Please sit here." I said, feeling a thrilling flush.

"No, no, no" The doctor wiped his eyes with a huge clean white handkerchief. "I cannot sit. I am too happy to tell you that your case has troubled me so that I send the results to be read by expert in Geneva. It has been misjudged by an imbecile at the

Berne Clinique. He is no longer with the Clinique, rest assured. You have never had a brain tumor, Madame Sargent, never, never, never. What you have is called a meningioma. It might have already disappeared." He tried to continue but instead, shrugged with happiness. To deliver news of this magnitude was new to him and he was overwhelmed. Stevie sat in her chair and stared at the doctor, stunned.

"You will live a very long time, Madame Sargent, I am sure."

Stevie, her eyes huge with wonder, her mouth agape, tried to stand to come over to me, but her legs wouldn't work, so she reached her hand out to me and we held hands across the flaming hearth. I stared at the doctor, breathing through my mouth, but I couldn't speak either. A clarion of tumult was ringing through my head.

When he found his voice, he waved his hand and handkerchief, "Such a mistake! Signora, I am so very sorry for the anguish we have caused you." He added, gravely,

"You know people in your circumstance at these sad times have done some crazy things."

"Is that right, Dottore?" I said. I touched the small brown bottle of amphodons inert in the bottom of my pocket.

"Oh, yes, sir, fatality has not been out of the question."

When I was able to, I smiled.

And while the embarrassed Doctor Pontebianco stood at the deep-set small window pretending to watch the rain, I pulled Stevie to her feet and took her in my arms as the room careened around us, becoming a carousel. "I'll love you forever, Stevie." My mouth found hers.

Our mouths joined in a kiss that neither of us had ever known. Outside, the sun smashed through the clouds and bejeweled the dripping trees and flooded the room in yellow-gold light.

Poor Doctor Pontebianco no longer tried to avert his eyes as he openly watched the lovers, many of his huge teeth visible below his ornamental moustache, grinning, his cheeks wet with tears.

"Oh, Goaty, I'll love you ever after, my darling," Stevie whispered against my lips. Suddenly, with a surge of love-born strength, I lifted her off the stone floor and held her aloft in the new sunlight.

"It's all that matters!" I called out to the listening sky.

THE END.

ACKNOWLEDGEMENT

I wish to express my sincere thanks to Doug Lane for his proofreading and his detailed, insightful editing of the book.

For his constant encouragement and invaluable suggestions, I extend my thanks to Colby Chester.

And finally I thank my dear brother, David, who in the midst of his very busy (award winning) art exhibits in Ireland, gave his time and talent to design another book cover for me. Without their generous help this book would have floundered.

Madeleine McKay

About the Author

❧◦❧

Gardner McKay, Author and Playwright, was born in Manhattan, 1932. His early years were spent in France, New York, Connecticut and Kentucky.

At age fifteen, he published his first story. Over the next several years he received many awards, including The Drama Critics Circle Award, the Sydney Carrington Prize, National Regional Theatre Award of Canada and three National Endowment for the Arts grants for playwriting. His plays include: *Sea Marks, Masters of the Sea, Toyer, Untold Damage,* and *In Order of Appearance.*

His novel *Toyer* won critical acclaim upon its release in 1998. Gardner's weekly radio show "Stories on the Wind," was broadcast on Hawaii Public Radio from 1995—2001. He taught playwriting at UCLA and at USC. He also taught in Juneau, Alaska and at the University of Hawaii at Manoa. He was a professional skipper, sculptor, photographer and actor, as well as a drama critic for the *Los Angeles Herald Examiner*. In addition to all that, he raised African lions.

During his final year, Gardner wrote his memoir: *Journey Without A Map*, which was published posthumously. As were *The Kinsman,* a novel, published in 2012 and in 2015 his novel *Trompe l'Oeil* and also a novella *Ten Bloomsbury Square:* And in 2017, *Stories on the Wind,* an antholgy of short stories, volume I.

98465519R00140

Made in the USA
Columbia, SC
26 June 2018